Bond

No.1 for exam success

Maths and Non-verbal Reasoning

Assessment Practice for the **CEM** test

Age 9–10 Year 5

Alison Primrose

OXFORD
UNIVERSITY PRESS

OXFORD
UNIVERSITY PRESS

Great Clarendon Street, Oxford OX2 6DP

Oxford University Press is a department of the University of Oxford.
It furthers the University's objective of excellence in research, scholarship,
and education by publishing worldwide. Oxford is a registered trade mark
of Oxford University Press in the UK and in certain other countries

British Library Cataloguing in Publication Data
Data available

978-0-19277983-0

10 9 8 7 6 5 4 3 2 1

Paper used in the production of this book is a natural, recyclable
product made from wood grown in sustainable forests.
The manufacturing process conforms to the environmental
regulations of the country of origin.

Printed in China

Acknowledgements

Content Development Adviser: Michellejoy Hughes
Content Development Adviser and Reviewer: Jane Cooney
Additional material by Michellejoy Hughes
Page make-up: Integra Software Services
Cover illustrations: Lo Cole
Illustrations: Integra Software Services and Tech-Set Ltd, Gateshead

Although we have made every effort to trace and contact
all copyright holders before publication this has not been
possible in all cases. If notified, the publisher will rectify
any errors or omissions at the earliest opportunity.

Contents

Two further Mixed Papers are available online at **www.bond11plus.co.uk**

Welcome

The CEM Select Entrance Assessment is a computer-based 11[+] test that assesses a child in verbal, non-verbal and mathematical reasoning. It covers English and maths topics that a child will be familiar with from the National Curriculum, but, in common with other 11[+] exams, supplements these with verbal reasoning and non-verbal reasoning questions. What makes the CEM exam different from other assessments is the way that it blends English and verbal reasoning in one test and then maths and non-verbal reasoning in another, rather than offering four separate tests. CEM (Centre for Evaluation and Monitoring) do not offer their own practice materials or past papers and deliberately vary the contents of the exam each year, which means that the CEM 11[+] is often seen as being more challenging to prepare for.

All Bond 11[+] materials are effective preparation for CEM Select and develop the skills and aptitudes that a child needs for success, but CEM-specific titles, like this one, are designed to hone the flexibility of approach essential to overcoming the particular challenges of the CEM test. The Bond system provides learning, information and consolidation so that children have an extended, rich education. Our aim is to familiarise children with the type of questions they will find in the exam and to give them the transferable skills that will allow a child to attempt any question in any exam.

Bond offers a complete, flexible programme of preparation materials that you can adapt to your child's specific needs and to the requirements of the exam, or exams. There are timings provided for each paper. Children can complete a paper in one sitting, or in smaller sections. The CEM online exam has an additional 25% time allowance for candidates needing additional support. If this applies to your child, add an extra 25% for each timed section.

Why Use a Book to Prepare for an Online Test?

Since 2022, the CEM Select 11[+] test has only been offered as a computer-based assessment. Whilst it is worth spending some test-practice time using an online platform such as Bond Online to gain familiarity with completing assessments through a digital interface, books remain a highly effective way of developing the skills necessary for success in a structured way whilst reducing screen time.

Not Just for the CEM Select 11[+]

This book has been designed to be especially effective preparation for the rigours of the CEM 11[+] test, but the skills can be applied to any 11[+] exams or independent school entrance exams and are also great for engaged pupils looking for an extra challenge or to ready themselves for secondary school.

Remember to keep checking in with your school of choice so that you know which exam they use – schools do change their exam boards from time to time. If your exam board does change, all is not lost. This book will still have been good preparation for other exam boards.

KEY STUDY SKILLS

Working towards an entrance exam can be an exciting challenge. It is the chance to learn new things and to prepare for secondary school. Here are some tips to help you:

• Create a study schedule so that you have a regular routine

• Balance short bursts of practice with longer assessment papers

• Create a quiet study space with pencils, an eraser, paper for working out, your books and a notebook for copying strategies in. If you study in different places, keep everything in a box that you can take with you

• Write down strategies to solve new topics, but don't forget to revise and consolidate

• Limit distractions such as television, technology and games when you are studying

• Remember that errors are useful. They are part of the journey to success.

A Note for Parents

Parents have a crucial role in helping children and motivating them. Here are some ways that you can really make a difference.

• Check your child is working at the right level. The goal is being able to score 85% on average. It's demotivating if they can't complete questions. It is also important that they work through the system so that they are at the right level for the exam at the right time.

• Mark work promptly and go through errors. If papers have not been marked, a child has no idea how they are doing or whether they are repeating the same mistake.

• Use the Bond Handbooks to help your child understand new techniques.

• Limit the range of homework you give your child. The best results are achieved by a system that gradually increases in difficulty. Completing lots of books and papers doesn't guarantee your child's success and often creates stress.

• If your child is struggling with something specific, add additional support in that area. If your child is not achieving an 85% average in CEM-specific books you can also use other subject-specific Bond Assessment Practice books at the same level or Bond 10 Minute Tests for consolidation.

• Communication is key. Remain positive and encourage your child to focus on the positive. No exam is going to ask for 100% so pushing for that is unrealistic and stressful.

• If your child is constantly struggling, be realistic over whether a selective education is the right choice for your child now. Many children move to a selective school for their GCSEs or A levels so not going to a selective school now doesn't mean they never will. It is about finding the best school for your child.

How to Use This Book

This book includes many step-by-step techniques for solving different question types. If further support is needed it can be used alongside one or more of the Bond Handbooks, which offer insights into the full range of questions that might occur in the exam.

- The first section of the book is the Learning Papers that focus on key skills with worked examples then lots of questions for consolidation.

- The second section of the book is Mixed Papers so that children continue to consolidate and do not forget what they have learnt. Go online at **www.bond11plus.co.uk** and register for free resources to get two additional Mixed Papers.

- The final section includes two full Test Papers, which can be broken down into shorter sections for more focussed practice, or can be used as full mock tests for that all-important exam practice.

- There is an 11⁺ study guide at the back of the book with some useful hints and tips.

- There are fully worked out answers to explain how an answer has been reached.

Logic, Sequences and Grids

KEY SKILL

When looking for patterns in number sequences, start by noting the difference between each of the terms in the sequence. This will indicate the pattern that is being followed.

E.g.   3   10   17   24   ?

so +7 will give the next term 24 + 7 = 31

+7   +7   +7

When looking for sequences in shapes or patterns look carefully at the number, size and shading of the different elements. Ask yourself these sorts of questions:

- Does the number of lines or size of a shape increase or decrease?
- Are any elements alternating?
- Are any shapes rotating?
- Does the shading style of any part follow a pattern?

WORKED EXAMPLES

Which pattern completes the larger shape or grid? Underline the answer.

a   b   c   d   e

Which picture or pattern on the bottom row comes next in the pattern on the top row? Underline the answer.

Maths Sequences

1 What number comes next?

a 120, 109, 98, 87, ...

b 8, 15, 22, 29, 36, ...

c 12 090, 11 080, 10 070, ...

d 79, 74, 69, 64, 59, 54, ...

TOP TIP!

If the numbers in a sequence increase in size, then they will have been added to or multiplied. If they decrease, they will have been subtracted from or divided.

Key skills highlight the topic then offer tips and strategies to succeed. It is important to read this carefully so that you understand the techniques needed.

Worked examples offer support so that a child understands what to do and what to look out for. Read this carefully. It may help with revision if you copy the worked example into a notebook so that you know what to do.

Timed activity for children to consolidate their skills in an appropriate time.

KEY MATHS AND NON-VERBAL REASONING SKILLS

The Bond Maths and Non-verbal Reasoning Book covers the elements that are found in the CEM online 11+ exam, but is useful for all CEM-style online and written 11+ exams. The Learning Papers cover the following key skills:

- **Mathematics** – a wide range of topics including data, arithmetic and problem solving
- **NVR** – including rotational, reflection, series, sequences and similarities
- **Spatial** – including cubes/nets, 2D and 3D shapes, transformations, and shape combinations.

The Mixed Papers ensure the key skills are consolidated thoroughly then the Test Papers give children the opportunity to get used to the exam process as a natural progression of each book. Don't forget that a rounded education is key. Get used to reading graphs, timetables and charts. Try doing Sudoku and number games, play online games like Tetris or Snake and have a go at some logic and number puzzles – Bond has a number of puzzle books to help make this more fun. Create an ongoing list of strategies or techniques such as 'how to find volume' or 'how to multiply with decimals' to extend your maths skills.

Each book is part of the Bond system with books increasing gradually in difficulty. Once your child has completed this book, there is a clear progression in starting the next book level if your child has an average of 85% in this book. If they have achieved an average of 70% – 85%, then another book at the same level as this one will provide further support. If your child has achieved less than a 70% average, then moving down a level will be most useful. Once your child has developed the skills needed at a lower level, they can move up with confidence.

Learning Papers

Special Numbers and Place Value

Build your confidence with number work by sharpening your knowledge of types of number, number bonds and multiplication tables. Secure knowledge of your times tables will help you to identify factors and multiples quickly. A **factor** of a number is a whole number which divides exactly into another larger number, e.g. the factors of 8 are 1, 2, 4 and 8. When two whole numbers are multiplied together, the answer is a **multiple** of both numbers, e.g. 24 is a **multiple** of 3 and 8.

A **prime number** is a number that can only be divided exactly by 1 and the number itself. The first ten prime numbers are 2, 3, 5, 7, 11, 13, 17, 19, 23, 29. Numbers that are not prime are called **composite numbers** and are divisible by more than two numbers.

A **square number** is a number multiplied by itself. Work out all of the square numbers from 1 to 400 (1 × 1, 2 × 2, 3 × 3 and so on up to 20 × 20). Write them down in colour so that you can recognise them quickly.

A **cubed number** is a number multiplied by itself twice – remember 1 times itself is always 1, so 1 is both a square number and a cubed number. Try to remember and recognise these cubic numbers:

2 × 2 × 2 = **8**	3 × 3 × 3 = **27**	4 × 4 × 4 = **64**
5 × 5 × 5 = **125**	6 × 6 × 6 = **216**	10 × 10 × 10 = **1000**

You need to know the value of a digit wherever it appears in a number. Understanding place value is important for ordering and rounding. **Rounding** is the process of simplifying a number to make calculations easier. If the digit being rounded to is followed by a digit that is 5 or more, it increases by 1. If it is followed by a digit that is 4 or less, it stays the same.

Estimating an answer in your head can help you check that your answer is sensible.

TOP TIP!

Addition and multiplication always give a larger number in the answer.

Subtraction and division always give a smaller number in the answer

WORKED EXAMPLES

Order these numbers from smallest to biggest.

37524.2	37542	35424.2	37452
35424.2	**37452**	**37524.2**	**37542**

When ordering numbers, start by looking at the number of columns, and then the value of the digits in each column, starting with the highest value column. It can be helpful to put the numbers in a table, lining them up in the column headings, taking care with decimal points.

Here, all the numbers start with 3, so look at the next column. One of the numbers here is smaller than 7, so that is the smallest number. If the digits are the same in the column move on until there is a difference.

TTH	TH	H	T	O		th
3	7	5	2	4	.	2
3	7	5	4	2		
3	5	4	2	4	.	2
3	7	4	5	2		

The temperature is 6°C and falls 13 degrees. What is the temperature now? **–7°C**

If the temperature is 6°C and it falls 13 degrees, the new temperature will be –7°C. A fall of 6°C takes the temperature down to 0°C or freezing point, and then the fall of a further 7°C takes the temperature down to –7°C.

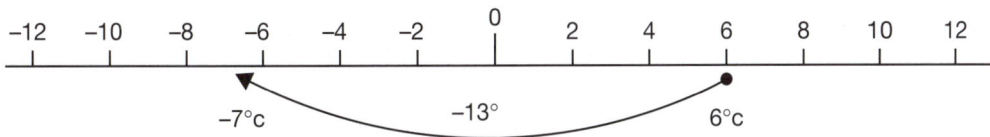

30 mins

Place Value

1 What is the temperature 15° below 6°C? .... ☐ 1

2 Write the number 8 104 519 in words.

   .... ☐ 1

3 Write four million, thirty-two thousand, three hundred and two in digits.

   .... ☐ 1

4 **Round** each of the following numbers to:

	the nearest hundred	the nearest ten
a 98 099	....	....
b 191 891	....	....

☐ 2

5 **Round** 49 598.7 to the

a nearest ten: ....

b nearest thousand: ....

c nearest whole number: 3

6 Order the following numbers by rewriting them from smallest to biggest.

978 794   980 212   975 936   980 203

.... 1

7 What is 25 plus 32 minus 60?

.... 1

8 One night the temperature fell to –21°C. It went up 6 degrees during the day but then fell 11 degrees the next night. What was the temperature on the second night?

.... 1

9 One year the population of a town was recorded as 24 560. It increased by 2078 the following year, and a further 1005 in the next year. What was the new total population?

.... 1

Factor and Multiples

10 Which of these numbers is a **factor** of 34?

2, 3, 4, 5, 6, 7, 8, 9 1

11 Give another three pairs of **factors** for the number 48:

1 and 48, 2 and 24, ..., ..., ... 3

12 Give three **multiples** of 15 between 31 and 100. ...., ..., ... 1

13 Which of the following numbers are not **multiples** of 6? Underline them.

      48   64   72   98   106

14 A concert hall has 32 rows of seats with 25 seats in each row. How many seats are there all together?

....

15 A school of 325 pupils make up teams of 7 for a competition, how many complete teams will there be and how many pupils will be left out?

....

16 All of these numbers can be divided by 2. What other whole number can they all be divided by without leaving any remainder?

      36   54   78   102   ....

Square, Cubed, Composite and Prime Numbers

17 $4^2 +$ .... $= 147 \div 7$

18 What is the value of $5^2 + 8^2$? ....

19 Which of these is a **prime** number? 4, 10, 13, 15, 18, 21 ....

20 Underline the **prime** numbers and circle the **composite** numbers.

      2   13   9   27   31   17

21 Which of these numbers is not a **cubed** number? Underline them.

      1   27   125   369   512   1000

22 What is 4^3? ....

1

1

1

1

1

2

1

3

1

1

Total
30

Logic, Sequences and Grids

KEY SKILL

When looking for patterns in number sequences, start by noting the difference between each of the terms in the sequence. This will indicate the pattern that is being followed.

E.g.   3   10   17   24   ?

+7   +7   +7

so +7 will give the next term 24 + 7 = 31

When looking for sequences in shapes or patterns look carefully at the number, size and shading of the different elements. Ask yourself these sorts of questions:

- Does the number of lines or size of a shape increase or decrease?

- Are any elements alternating?

- Are any shapes rotating?

- Does the shading style of any part follow a pattern?

WORKED EXAMPLES

Which pattern completes the larger shape or grid? Underline the answer.

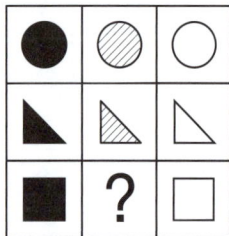

a   b   c   d   e

Which picture or pattern on the bottom row comes next in the pattern on the top row? Underline the answer.

?

a   b   c   d   e

As with number sequences, in NVR sequences the terms may be in a simple step-by-step progression and may often have two or more progressions happening. Here there is a pattern in the shapes (circle, triangle, square) and in the shading (diagonal stripes, no shading). So the next term is a circle with diagonal stripes, which is **option a**.

Maths Sequences

1 What number comes next?

    a 120, 109, 98, 87, ...

    b 8, 15, 22, 29, 36, ...

    c 12 090, 11 080, 10 070, ...

    d 79, 74, 69, 64, 59, 54, ...

    e 10, 11, 13, 16, 20, 25, ...

> ### TOP TIP!
> If the numbers in a sequence increase in size, then they will have been added to or multiplied. If they decrease, they will have been subtracted from or divided

NVR Grids

Which pattern completes the larger shape or grid? Underline the answer.

2

a   b   c   d   e

3

a   b   c   d   e

4

a   b   c   d   e

5

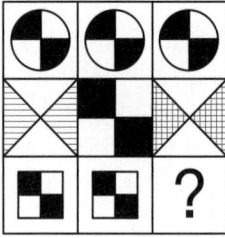

a   b   c   d   e

6

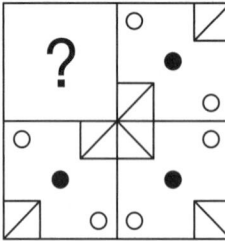

a   b   c   d   e

7

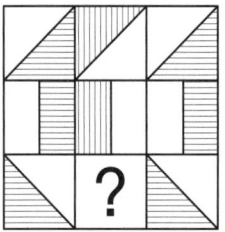

a   b   c   d   e

8

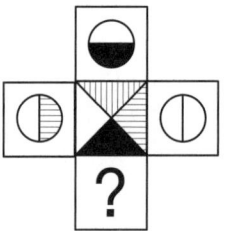

a   b   c   d   e

9

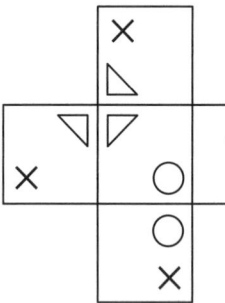

a   b   c   d   e

10

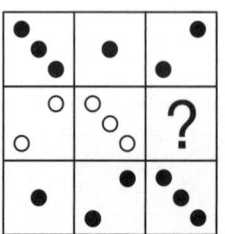

a   b   c   d   e

9

NVR Sequences

Which picture or pattern on the bottom row comes next in the pattern on the top row?
Underline the answer.

11

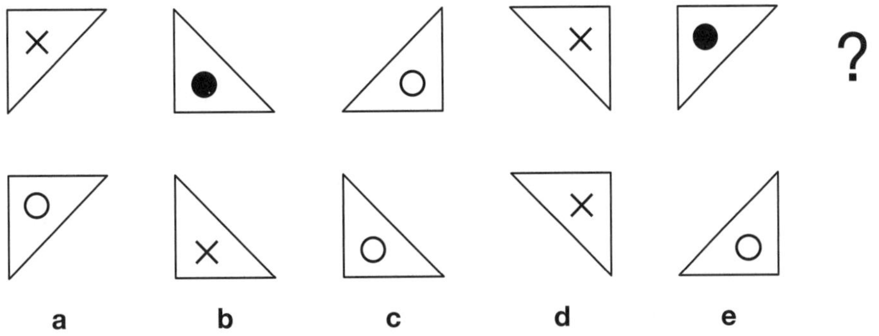

a   b   c   d   e

12

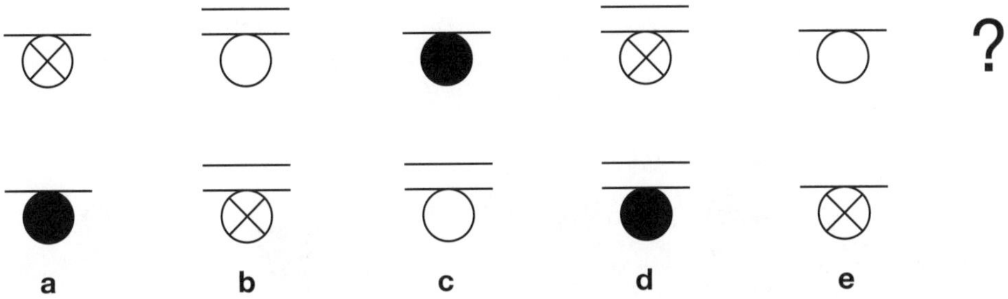

a   b   c   d   e

13

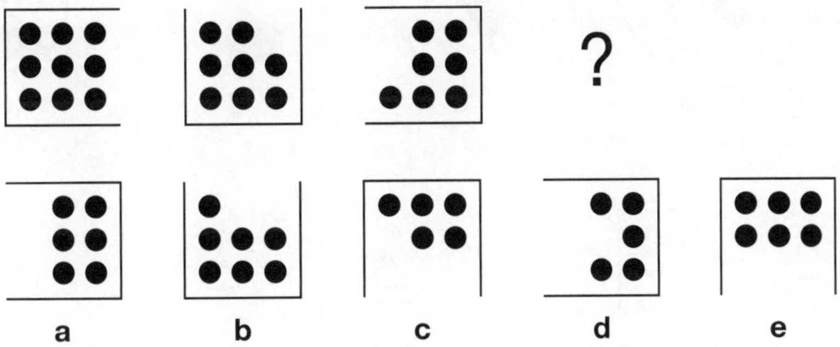

a   b   c   d   e

14

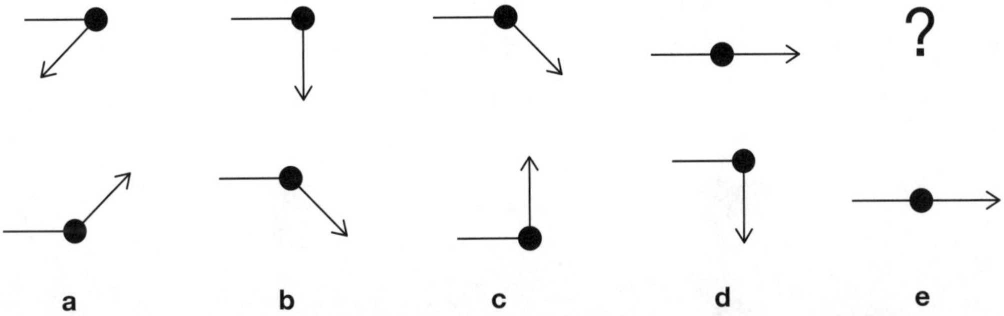

a   b   c   d   e

15

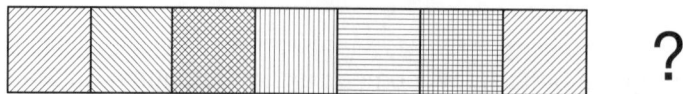

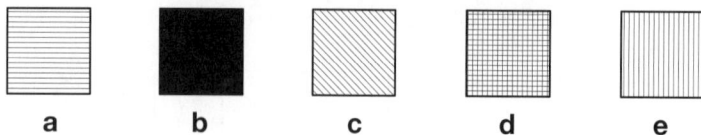

a   b   c   d   e

16

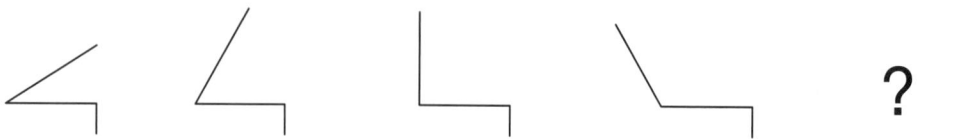

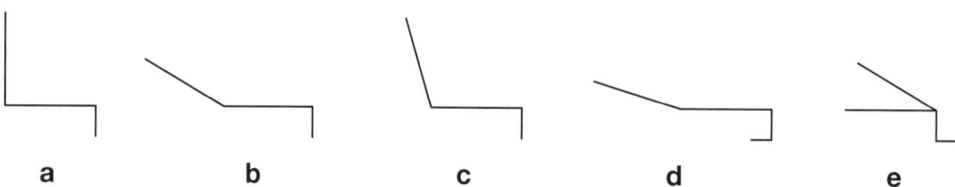

a   b   c   d   e

17

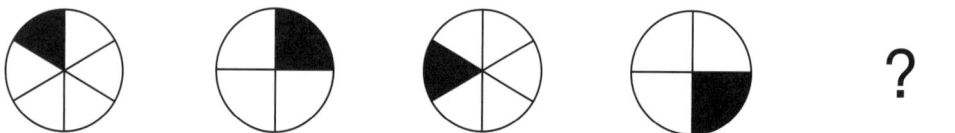

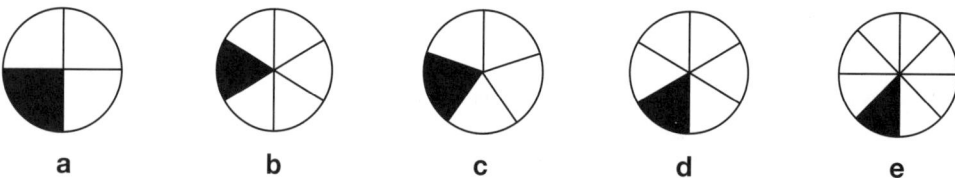

a   b   c   d   e

18

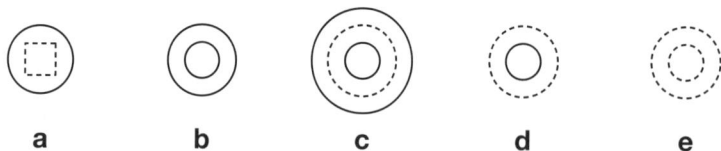

a   b   c   d   e

19

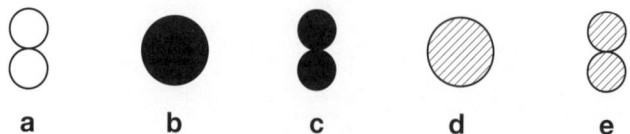

a   b   c   d   e

Words and Logic Problems

20 Sal needs to have a 5ml dose of medicine 3 times a day. She is given a 135ml bottle of the medicine. For how many days will the medicine last?

.... ☐ 1

21 The numbers on the left are fed into these function machines.

Complete the missing numbers.

a 15 $\boxed{\times 3}$ .... $\boxed{+7}$ ....

b 103 $\boxed{\times 5}$ .... $\boxed{-7}$ .... ☐ 2

22 A recipe needs 150g butter, 120g sugar and 250g of flour to make 24 biscuits.
If Tara uses 250g of butter:

a How much sugar does she need? ....

b How many biscuits will her mixture make? .... ☐ 2

23 Find the missing numbers or symbols in this grid.

3	a	b	=	18
×	■	–	■	c
d	–	4	=	4
=	■	=	■	=
e	–	2	=	f

> **TOP TIP!**
> Look for a row or column that only has one piece of information missing and start there

a .... **b** .... **c** ....

d .... **e** .... **f** .... ☐ 2

24 A sailing competition has 18 small boats, 32 medium-sized boats and 11 larger ones setting off on a race. Five boats capsize and six have to abandon the race. How many boats complete the race?

.... ☐ 1

25 A farmer has a flock of 210 sheep. He needs one sack of food to feed seven sheep for a week. If he has 240 sacks, for how many weeks can he feed the sheep?

.... ☐ 1

Total
32

Number Skills

KEY SKILL

Simplifying fractions

Fractions can be simplified when both the top number (the numerator) and the bottom number (the denominator) can be divided exactly by the same whole number.

If they cannot be divided by the same number then the fraction is in its simplest form, e.g.

$\frac{3}{6}$ Both numbers can be divided exactly by 3 giving $\frac{1}{3}$

$\frac{7}{10}$ There are no numbers that divide exactly into 7 and 11, so this is in its simplest form

The denominator, or bottom number in a fraction, shows you how many parts the whole has been divided into.

The numerator, or top number in a fraction, shows you how many of the equal-sized parts of the whole are being considered.

When adding or subtracting fractions, all of the fractions need to have the same denominator, then the numerators are simply added or subtracted according to the calculation required. To find a fraction equivalent to another fraction, multiply the numerator and the denominator by the same number.

Fractions, decimals and percentages

To convert fractions to percentages, multiply by 100. To convert a percentage to a fraction, write the percentage as a fraction with 100 as the denominator and simplify. As percentages are in hundredths, they can easily be written as decimal fractions using the tenths and hundredths column.

Working with decimals

When calculating with decimal numbers remember to keep the decimal point in line when doing addition or subtraction calculations.

WORKED EXAMPLES

$$\frac{2}{3} + \frac{1}{4} + \frac{5}{6} = 1\frac{3}{4}$$

Step 1: Convert all fractions to 12ths by finding equivalent fractions so that all the denominators are the same. $\frac{2}{3} = \frac{8}{12}$ $\frac{1}{4} = \frac{3}{12}$ $\frac{5}{6} = \frac{10}{12}$

Step 2: Then add the numerators. $8 + 3 + 10 = 21$

Step 3: Convert $\frac{21}{12}$ to a mixed number and simplify the fraction if possible.

To change an improper fraction into a mixed number, first divide the denominator into the numerator to find how many wholes can be made. Then express the remainder as a fraction.

$$\frac{21}{12} = 1\frac{9}{12} = 1\frac{3}{4}$$

51.73 + 6.5 =

5	1	·	7	3
	6	·	5	
5	8	·	2	3

Round and estimate in your head: 52 + 7 is 59

Check – is the answer near 59?
Yes, so the decimal point is in the correct place.

51.73 – 6.5 =

⁴5	¹1	·	7	3
	6	·	5	
4	5	·	2	3

Round and estimate in your head: 52 – 7 = 45

Check – is answer near 45?
Yes, so the decimal point is in the correct place.

Fractions

1 What is one-third of seven hundred and thirty-five? .... □ 1

2 In a jar of 100 beads, half are red and a quarter are blue.
One-fifth of the rest are white, and the remainder are green.

How many are green? .... □ 2

3 $\frac{3}{4}$ × .... = 210 □ 1

> **TOP TIP!**
> $\frac{3}{4}$ × ? is the same as $\frac{3}{4}$ of ?

4 Underline the odd one out:

$\frac{4}{28}$ $\frac{7}{49}$ $\frac{5}{35}$ $\frac{2}{7}$ □ 1

5 Underline the equivalent fractions:

$\frac{1}{6}$ $\frac{2}{8}$ $\frac{5}{10}$ $\frac{3}{12}$ $\frac{5}{20}$ $\frac{4}{5}$ □ 1

6 Order these fractions from the smallest to the largest:

$\frac{21}{27}$ $\frac{2}{9}$ $\frac{6}{18}$ $\frac{11}{99}$ .... □ 1

7 $\frac{2}{5} + \frac{4}{20} + \frac{3}{10} =$ .... □ 1

> **TOP TIP!**
> Remember to change the fractions so that they all have the same denominator

8 $\frac{11}{12} - \frac{1}{6} - \frac{1}{3} =$ .... □ 1

9   What is the total of $\frac{3}{7} + \frac{6}{7} + \frac{45}{7}$? Give your answer as a mixed number. . . . . `1` ☐

10 What is the total of $\frac{3}{4} + \frac{3}{6} + \frac{11}{12}$? Give your answer as a mixed number. . . . . `1` ☐

11 In a variety pack of twenty-eight biscuits, one-quarter
    are creams, one-seventh are ginger and half are chocolate.
    The remainder are wafers. How many are wafers?   . . . . `2` ☐

12 In a traffic survey, one-third of the cars counted
    were black. There were sixteen blue cars and four
    red cars in the rest of the survey. How many were black?   . . . . `1` ☐

Decimals

13 Sam buys some bread for £1.25, milk for £1.05 and 2 packets of biscuits for 89p each.

    a What is her total bill? . . . .

    b She gets 4 coins in change from a £5 note.
       What are they?   . . . . `2` ☐

14 3010.201 − 9.04 = ... `1` ☐

15 If 1 euro is worth 90p, what is the value in pounds of 7.50 euros? . . . . `1` ☐

16 A box set of 6 DVDs costs £24.99. Individually the DVDs cost £4.99. How much
    does Wain save by getting the box set rather than buying 6 separate DVDs?

    . . . . `2` ☐

17 402.55 + 40.04 = ... `1` ☐

18 What comes next in this sequence? 4.55, 4.70, 4.85, ... `1` ☐

19 Order these numbers from the smallest to the largest:

    0.947   1.029   1.027   0.989   0.972

    . . . . `1` ☐

TOP TIP!
To order numbers compare the digits in each column in turn starting at the left

20 Round these decimal numbers to the nearest whole number:

a 57.56 . . . .

b 409.64 . . . .

c 1099.91 . . . .

1

21 Round these decimal numbers to one decimal place:

a 4.673 . . . .

b 73.849 . . . .

c 29.958 . . . .

1

22 Complete the table.

		Divided by 100	Divided by 10	Divided by 1000
a	1257.3			
b	90.83			
c	484.9			

3

23 What number is the arrow pointing at on the number line below?

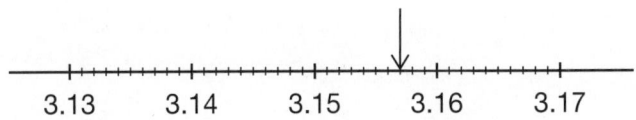

3.13   3.14   3.15   3.16   3.17

. . . .

1

Percentages

24 60% of 250 = ...

1

25 Mr Gold bought three items from a car boot sale for £22, £30 and £10 respectively.

He wants to sell them and make a 10% profit.

a How much must he sell them for altogether? . . . .

b If he actually sells the three together for £80, how much extra profit has he made over and above the 10%? . . . .

3

26 Abi gives 20% of £4 to her favourite charity.

How much does she give? . . . .

1

27 A litre of fuel used to cost £1.20.
The price goes up by 75%.

   a What is the new cost per litre?

....

Crackers cost £3.00. In a sale the price is reduced by 25%.

   b What is the reduced price?... **2**

28 **a** What is 40% of 280? .... **b** What is 70% of 450? **2**

Mixed Fractions, Decimals and Percentages

29 $\frac{1}{2}$ of 373.2 = ... **1**

30 A class of 20 children chose their favourite meal. Three-fifths of the children chose pizza, 10% chose burgers and the rest chose pasta.

   a What percentage chose pasta? ....

   b How many children chose pasta? **2**

31 Underline the odd one out.

   $\frac{3}{5}$ 60%   0.6 $\frac{7}{8}$ $\frac{6}{10}$ **1**

32 Underline the numbers that are the same as $\frac{3}{100}$:

   0.3 $\frac{1}{3}$ 0.03 $\frac{1}{33}$ 0.003   3%   **1**

33 Underline the numbers which have the same value:

   0.07   77% $\frac{7}{8}$ 7% $\frac{1}{7}$ 0.7   **1**

34 Which of these numbers have the same value? Underline the correct answer.

   $\frac{4}{7}$ $\frac{6}{10}$ 40% $\frac{4}{5}$ $\frac{75}{100}$ 0.8   **1**

Total **45**

Algebra and Codes

KEY SKILL

In algebra, an unknown number is often given a letter.

An equation is often given to enable you to find the value of the letter.

Remember that when you add, subtract, multiply or divide to solve the equation you must do the same to both sides of the equation in order for them to remain equal.

$$4x + 7 = 31$$

Subtract 7 from both sides to leave $4x$ on its own: $- 7 \quad - 7$

$$4x = 24$$

Then divide both sides by 4 to find the value of one x $\div 4 \quad \div 4$

$$x = 6$$

40 mins

Basic Algebra Skills

1 If $7a = 21$, what is the value of a? ....

2 If $12x = 84$, what is the value of x? ....

3 If $60 = 4y$, what is the value of y? ....

> **TOP TIP!**
>
> $4x$ means 4 times x, $3y$ means 3 times y and so on

4 If $x = 5$, what is the value of:

    a $7x - 4$ ....

    b $2x + 5x + 3$ ....

5 If $3y - 7 = 20$, what is the value of y? ....

6 If $y = 7$ and $z = 3$, what is the value of $2y + 3z$? ....

7 If $a = 2$, $b = 3$ and $c = 5$, what is the value of $3c + 2a + 3b$? ....

8 If $x = 10$, $y = 5$ and $z = 12$, what is the value of $2x + 3y + z$? ....

9   If the nth term in the following sequence is $3n$, what is the 7th term? 3, 6, 9, 12, ...

....   [1]

10 The equation for a sequence of numbers is $5n$. Give the value for the first three terms of the sequence.

....   [1]

11 If $a = 5$, solve the following equation: $a^2 + 10 =$ ....   [1]

WORKED EXAMPLE

Which code matches the shape or pattern given at the end of each line? Underline the answer.

AX	BY	CZ	AY	?	AZ	BX	CY	BZ	CX
					a	**b**	c	d	e

The first letter represents the shape (A is circle, B is triangle, C is square). The second letter represents the shading (X is diagonal stripes, Y is white, Z is black). The code is **b** BX

TOP TIP!

Look carefully at the shapes that have the same letter and identify the feature that is the same in them both. The other letters in that same position in the code will represent other forms of that same feature, e.g. other shapes or other shading styles

NVR Codes

Which code matches the shape or pattern given at the end of each line? Underline the answer.

12

AX	BY	CZ	CX	?	BX	AZ	BZ	CY	AY
					a	b	c	d	e

13

CX	CY	AY	BZ	?	AX	AZ	BX	BY	CZ
					a	b	c	d	e

14

DM EL DN FL ?

DL	EM	EN	FM	FN
a	b	c	d	e

15

AX BX AY CZ ?

AZ	BY	BZ	CX	CY
a	b	c	d	e

16

AY BZ BY CX ?

AX	AZ	BX	CY	CZ
a	b	c	d	e

17

AZ BX CZ AY ?

AX	BY	BZ	CX	CY
a	b	c	d	e

18

DR ES FT ER ?

ET	FR	FS	DS	DT
a	b	c	d	e

19

LA MB MA NC ?

LB	LC	MC	NB	NA
a	b	c	d	e

20

EA FB GC ED ?

GD	GA	EC	FA	GB
a	b	c	d	e

9

BIDMAS
Order of operations

The mnemonic BIDMAS can help you remember the order:

Brackets first

Indices next

Division and **M**ultiplication in order from left to right

Addition and **S**ubtraction elements again working from left to right

21 If a = 7, what is the value of (100 − 7a) + 20? .... | 1

22 (940 ÷ 5) − 10²? .... | 1

23 $\frac{1}{2}$ × 64 + ... = 40 | 1

24 If y = 7 and z = 3, what is the value of (10y ÷ 5) − z? .... | 1

25 (690 ÷ 3) + 4 = ... | 1

26 (152 ÷ 4) − 17 = ... | 1

27 (45 × 2) + (150 ÷ 5) = ... | 1

28 (156 ÷ 12) + (27 × 3) = ... | 1

29 3² + (91 ÷ 7) = ... | 1

30 (4² + 24) ÷ (3² + 1) = ... | 1

31 If a = 5 and b = 7, what is the value of (3a × 2) + b? .... | 1

32 If x = 2, y = 3, and z = 4, what is the value of (4z + 3) + (3y − 2) − (3x + 1)?

.... | 2

33 $\frac{32}{4}$ + (3 × 4) = ... | 1

Total
35

26

Shape, Space and Nets

KEY SKILL

Shapes

Learn the names of common 2D shapes and their properties:

Triangles have 3 sides – equilateral, right-angled, isosceles, scalene

Quadrilaterals have 4 sides – square, rectangle, parallelogram, rhombus, trapezium, kite

A **hexagon** has 6 sides and an **octagon** has 8 sides.

When working with 3D shapes the edges are where the sides of two faces meet, and remember that edges can be straight or curved.

The 'corners' where three or more faces meet are called vertices.

Be able to identify a cube, cuboid, cylinder, prism, pyramid and the nets that can be used to make them.

Angles

Acute angles are less than 90°

Right angles are 90°

Obtuse angles are more than 90 but less than 180°

Reflex angles are more than 180°

WORKED EXAMPLES

Which is the odd one out? Underline the answer.

Inspect each shape carefully – what features do they have in common? Look for features like shape, number of sides or lines, number or style of small shapes within the patterns. Look for shading patterns and check angles. Remember that all of the shapes except the odd one out will have the same features.

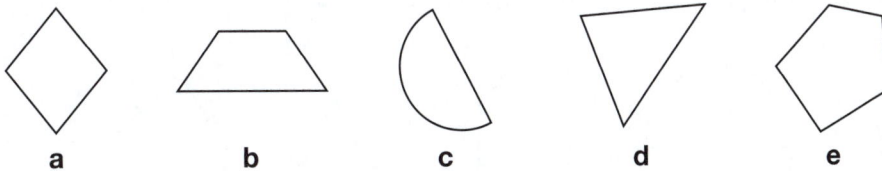

a   b   <u>c</u>   d   e

Which shape or pattern on the right belongs to the group on the left? Underline the answer.

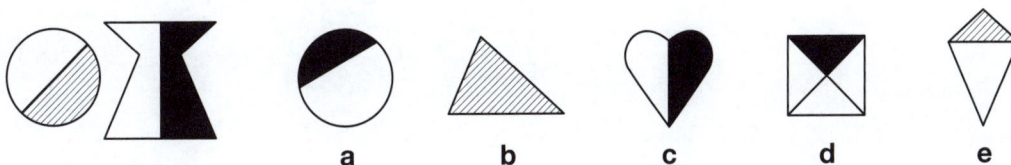

a   b   <u>c</u>   d   e

20 mins

Shape

1 How many rectangular **faces** are there on a **hexagonal prism?** 1

2 What solid shape is made if this **net** is folded up? 1

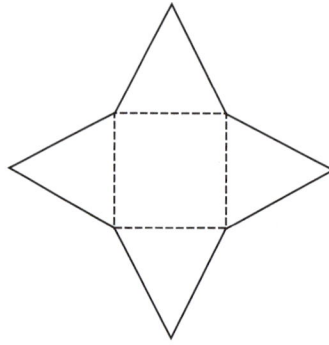

3 Name the 3D solid shapes that are made when these **nets** are folded up:

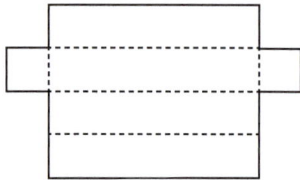 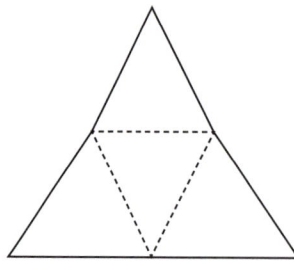 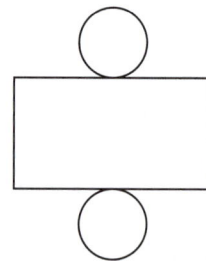

a .... **b** .... **c** 3

4 How many edges are there on a square-based pyramid? 1

5 Underline the 2D shapes that are regular polygons:

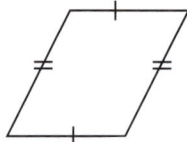 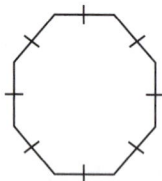  

a **b** **c** **d** **e** 1

6 Name the following quadrilaterals:

a  ....

b  ....

c  ....

Angles

7 What angle is formed between the large
and small hands of a clock when it is 3 o'clock? ....

8 If Tom is facing north and then turns clockwise to face
the south-east, through how many degrees does he turn? ....

9 Complete the following table – the first cell has been completed for you.

	35°	120°	60°	240°
Acute angle	**x**			
Obtuse angle				
Reflex angle				

10 Underline the obtuse angles:

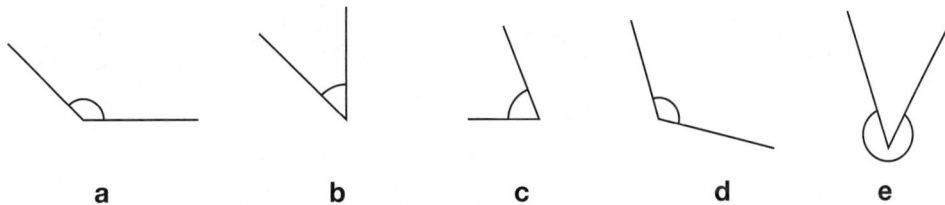

      a   **b**   **c**   **d**   **e**

11 How many degrees are there in an angle made up of three right angles?

  a ....   **b** What sort of angle is it? ....

12 What is the size of angle x? ....

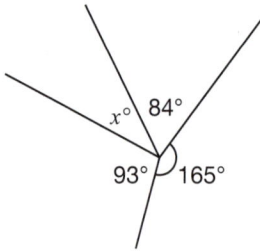

13 What is the size of angle y? ....

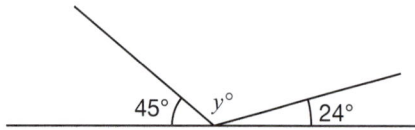

> **TOP TIP!**
>
> Remember your angle rules:
>
> - Angles round a point add up to 360°
> - Angles on a straight line add up to 180°
> - Angles in a triangle add up to 180°
> - Angles in a quadrilateral add up to 360°.

14 What is the sum of the internal angles of a parallelogram? ....

NVR Similar and Different Shapes

Which is the odd one out? Underline the answer.

15

| a | b | c | d | e |

16

| a | b | c | d | e |

17

| a | b | c | d | e |

18

| a | b | c | d | e |

Which shape or pattern on the right belongs to the group on the left? Underline the answer.

19

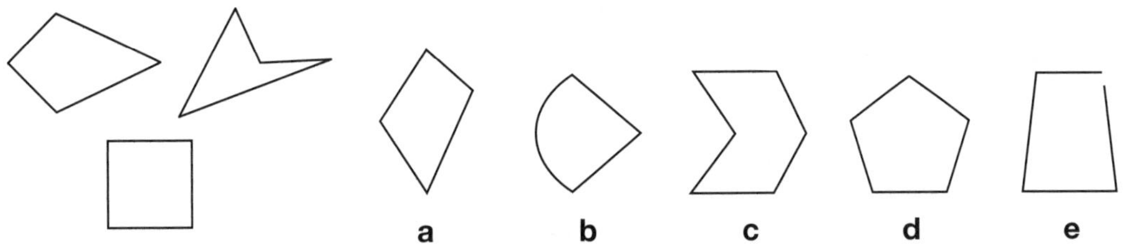

a   b   c   d   e

20

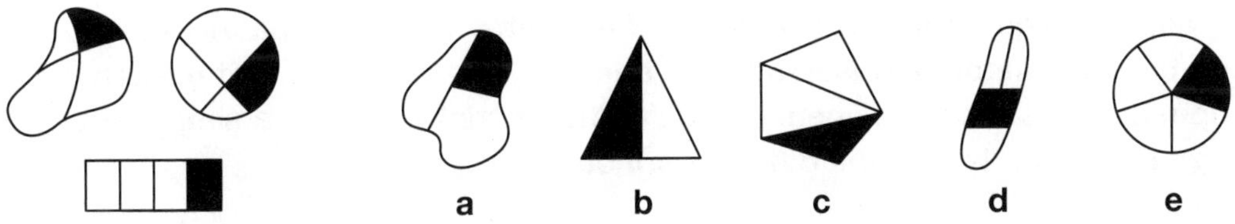

a   b   c   d   e

21

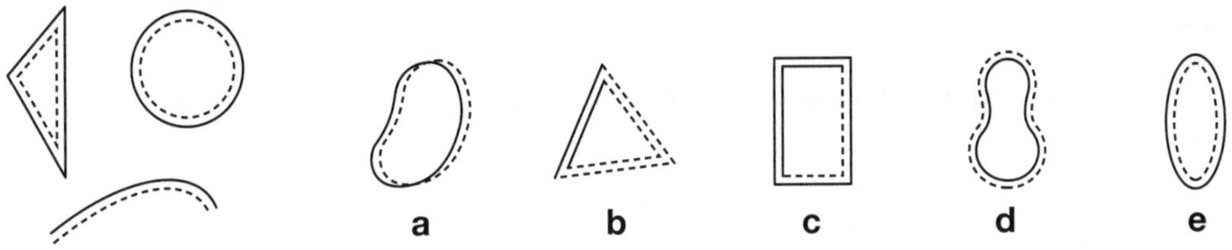

a   b   c   d   e

22

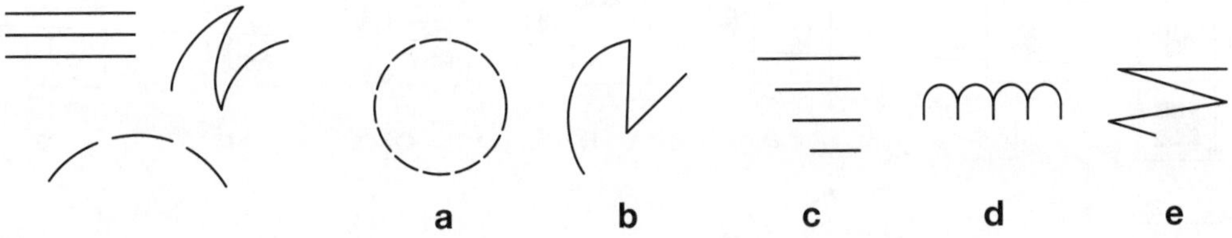

a   b   c   d   e

23

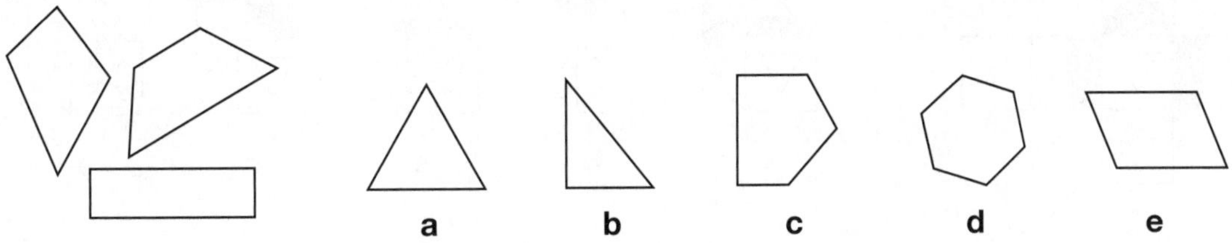

a   b   c   d   e

24

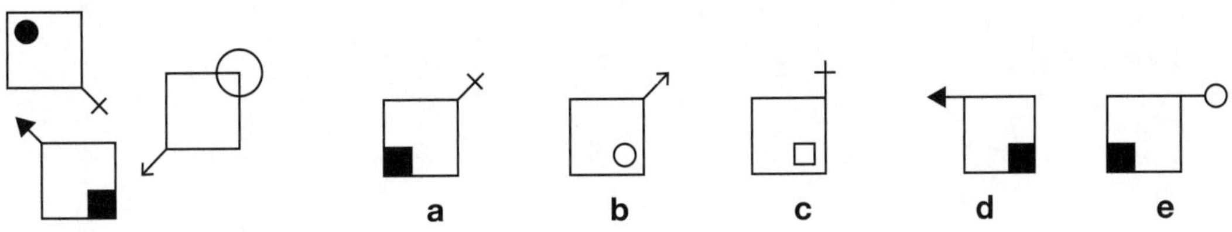

a   b   c   d   e

25

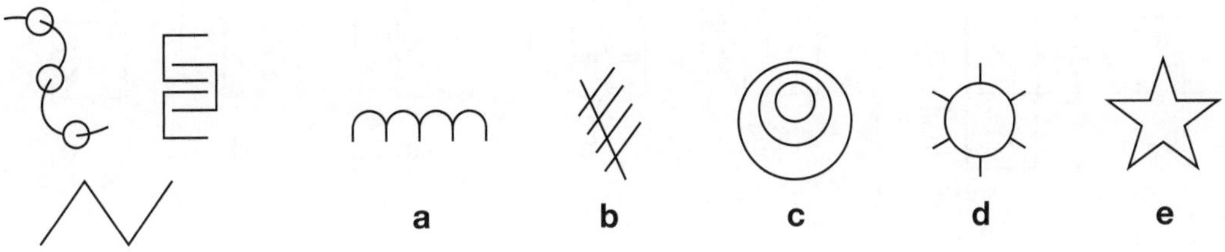

a   b   c   d   e

26

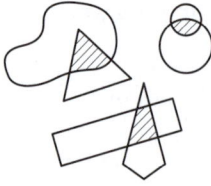

a   b   c   d   e

TOP TIPS!

Look at the direction of any specific shape such as an arrow and notice to which adjacent square/face it is pointing. Remember that three patterns in a row on the net cannot be observed from one side of a cube and that patterns on opposite faces won't be seen. If you find these tricky, cut out a simple net in rough paper and try out the different options

---

NVR Nets

Which of the following cubes can be made from the given net? Underline the answer.

27

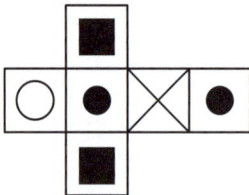

a   b   c   d   e

28

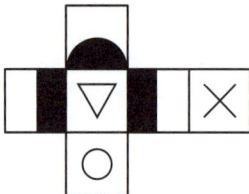

a   b   c   d   e

29

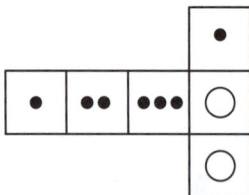

a   b   c   d   e

30

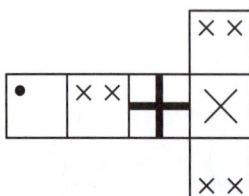

a   b   c   d   e

Total
36

Position and Direction

KEY SKILL

The **points of a compass** are often used to describe direction. Check that you know them, the angles that they form and the abbreviations normally used for each direction.

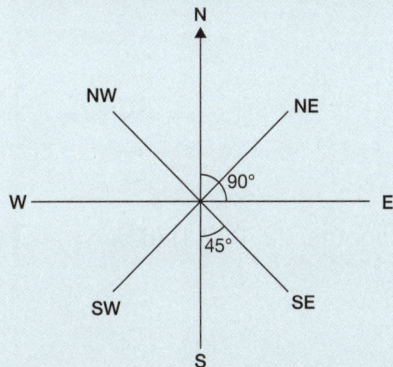

> **points of a compass**
> The directions shown on a compass. These include north, south, east, west and the points in-between: north-east, south-east, north-west and south-west

When looking for **symmetry** remember that the line of reflection is like a mirror line – the symmetrical image is the reflection in the mirror. If you find it hard to spot these practise by holding a plain mirror on the dotted line and inspecting the image in the mirror.

When a shape is **translated** in mathematics, it moves a left or right and/or up or down. The translated shapes look exactly the same as the original shape: it stays the same but its position moves. These types of questions will generally be given to you on squared paper, and the number of squares to be moved always gives the horizontal (x axis) number first then the vertical (y axis) number.

When a shape is **rotated** in mathematics this means an object is turned clockwise or anticlockwise around a given fixed point. That point does not change position. It may be the centre of a circle or the corner of a 2D shape.

WORKED EXAMPLE

Plot these pairs of points on the graph below joining them to make two separate straight lines, AB and CD. Give the coordinates of the point where the two lines cross over.

For the line AB, A is (1,5) B is (7,25) and for the line CD, C is (2,30) and D is (7,10).

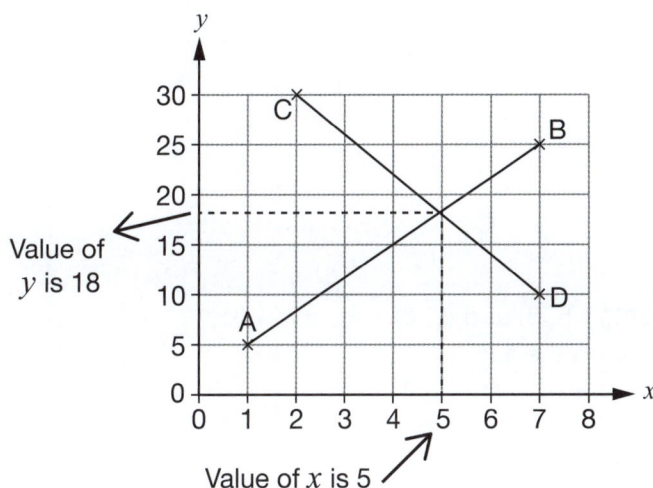

Value of y is 18

Value of x is 5

> ### TOP TIP!
> When plotting the points remember that the first number in a pair relates to the x axis and the second number relates to the y axis

coordinates (5, 18)

Direction

1   A ship sails north, then turns 45° in a **clockwise** direction.

> **clockwise** A rotational movement in the same direction as the movement of the hands of a clock

After another hour, the ship turns clockwise 90°.

In which compass direction is the ship now sailing? ....   `2`

2   Mark the following points on the graph below and join them together. (2,4) (2,1) (6,6)

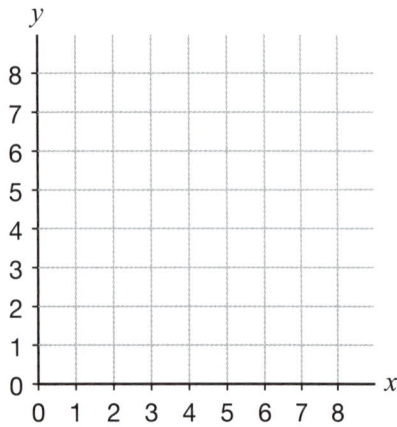

What type of triangle is it? ....   `2`

3   A weather vane pointing east is blown through 90 degrees in a **clockwise** direction.

In which direction is the weather vane now pointing? ....   `1`

Coordinates

4   Give the coordinates of the points A, B and C on the graph below.   `1`

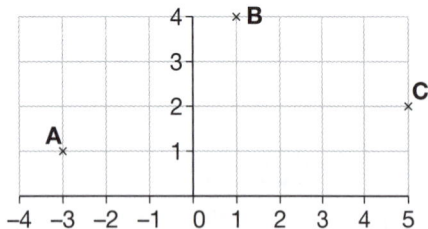

A....................   B.........................   C.........................

5   A straight line is drawn between the two points (-5, 3) and (2, 3).
Underline which of the following points will be on the line:

(2,2)   (-5,2)   (1,3)   (6,2)   (3,5)   `1`

34

Transformations

6 The triangle A, B, C is rotated 90 degrees **clockwise** about point B. What is the coordinate of point A in its new position? ....

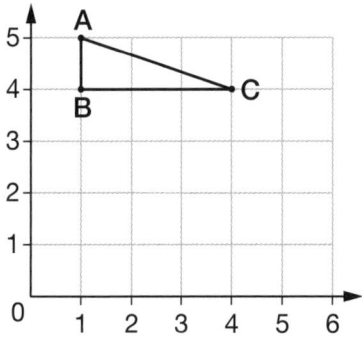

7 Draw the new position of the shape D, E, F, G when it is reflected in the *y* axis.

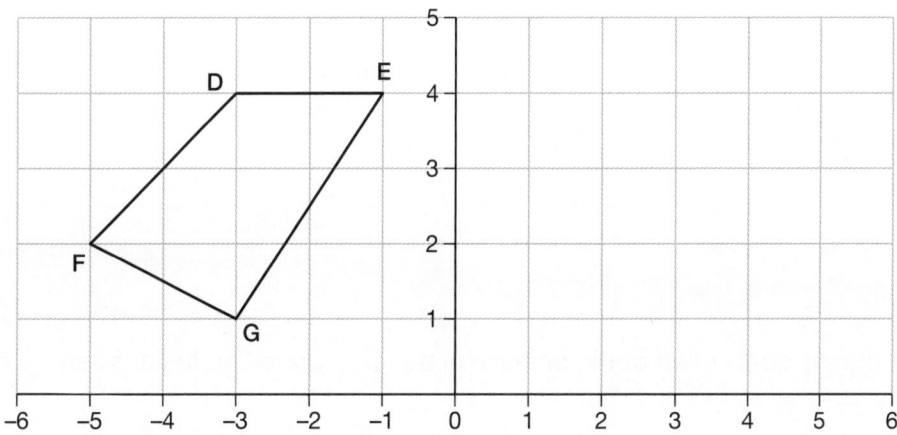

8 Draw a new triangle A' B' C' where the points A, B and C are translated by (*x* + 3, *y* + 2).

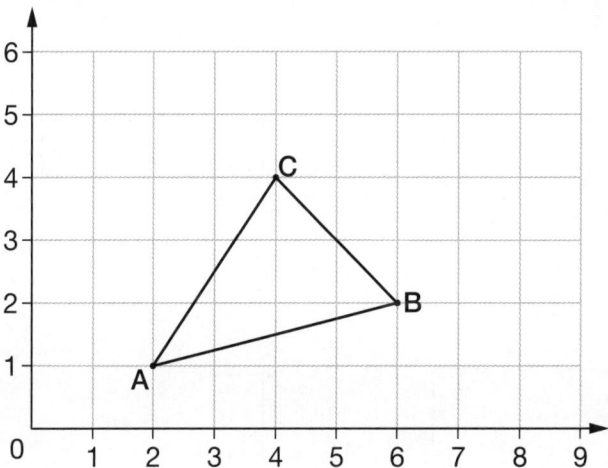

9 Complete the new pattern where the arrows rotate clockwise 45° and the black circles move 90° anticlockwise around the corners of the square:

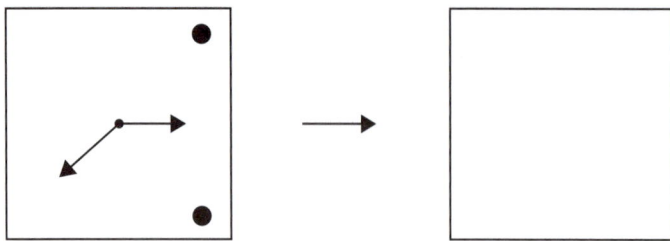

WORKED EXAMPLE

Which pattern on the right is a reflection of the pattern on the left? Underline the answer.

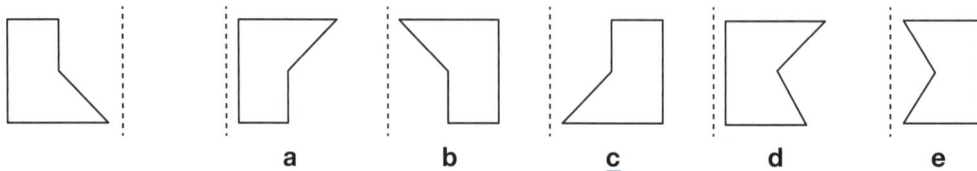

a   b   c   d   e

NVR Symmetry

Which pattern on the right is a reflection of the pattern on the left? Underline the answer.

10

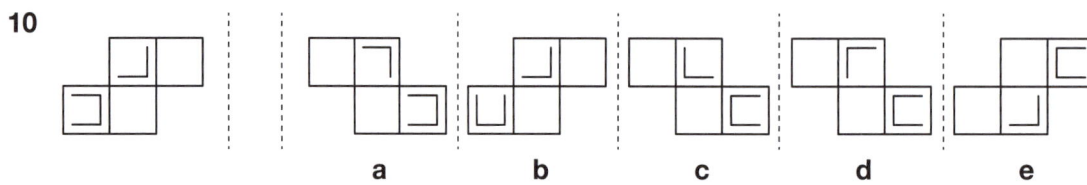

a   b   c   d   e

11

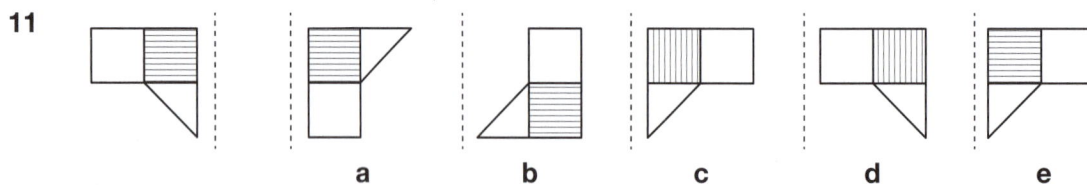

a   b   c   d   e

12

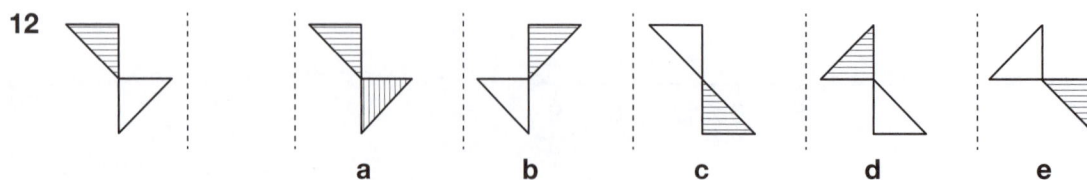

a   b   c   d   e

13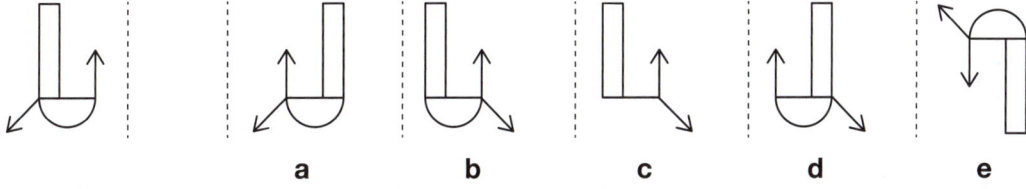

             a   b   c   d   e

14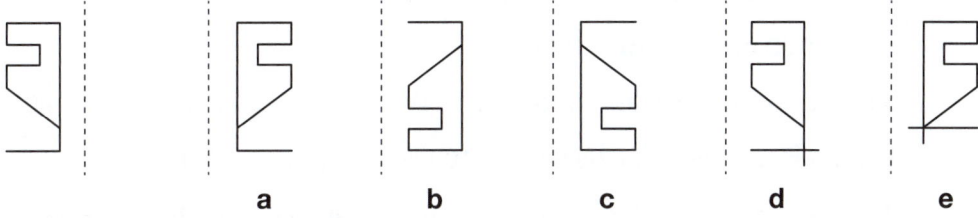

             a   b   c   d   e

15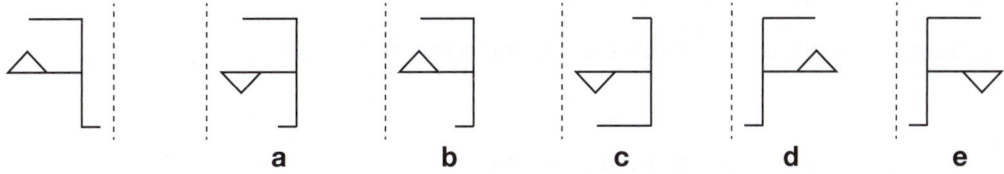

             a   b   c   d   e

16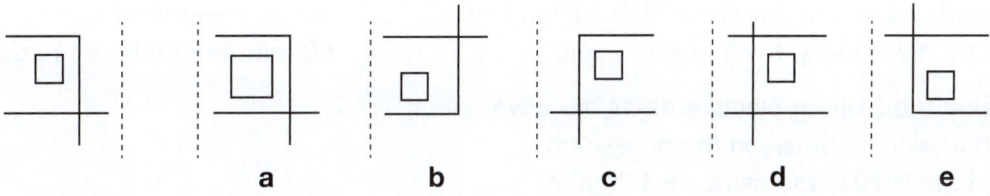

             a   b   c   d   e

17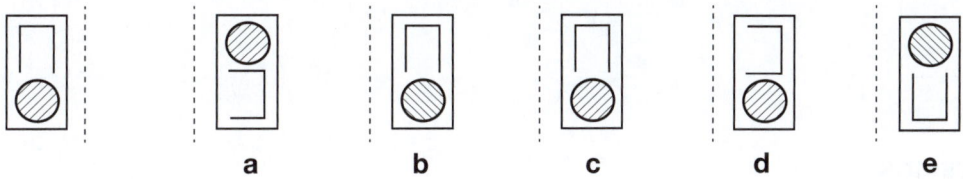

             a   b   c   d   e

18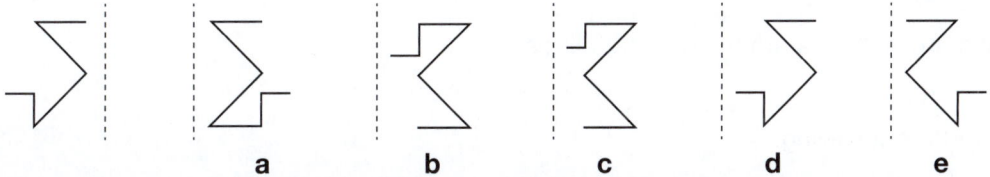

             a   b   c   d   e

Measurement and Pairs

KEY SKILL

When you are working with **metric measurements** check the number of zeros and/or decimal places very carefully:

Mass: **1 kg = 1000 g = 1 000 000 mg**   so ...   1 mg = 0.001 g = 0.000001 kg

Capacity: **1 l = 1000 ml so 1 ml = 0.001 l**

Length: **1 km = 1000 m = 1 000 000 mm**   so ...   1 mm = 0.001 m = 0.000001 km

Length also uses cm when 1 m = 100 cm, and 1 cm = 0.01 m

The old units of measurements, called imperial units, are rarely used. There are two sets that are worth knowing:

Length in feet and inches   12 inches = 1 foot

Mass in pounds and ounces 16 ounces = 1 lb (lb is the abbreviation for pounds)

Time

Hours, minutes and seconds are all measurements of time.

The time of day can be given using a.m. for times before midday and p.m. for times after midday, or they can be given using the 24-hour clock.

When using the 24-hour clock, 4 digits are always given, often with a : between the hours and minutes, e.g. 04:20 is the same as 4.20 a.m.

TOP TIP!

Remember 60 seconds make a minute and 60 minutes make an hour

40 mins

Conversions

1   2 m + 350 cm + 0.5 m = ... cm   1

2   How many millilitres are there in 3.03 litres?   1

3   Convert the following:

    a 4.2 litres to millilitres   1

    b 470 g to kilograms   1

4 How many metres is 4.5 km? .... m

5 Convert 72 350 m to kilometres .... km

6 Give the following times in the 24-hour clock format:

a 7.20 a.m. ....

b 3.30 p.m. ....

c 9.15 p.m. ....

7 Using a.m. or p.m., express the following 24-hour clock times in analogue format:

a 04:25 ....

b 13:20 ....

c 19:10 ....

8 If 1 kg is 2.2 lb, how many lbs is 7 kg? ....

9 If 39 inches is 1 metre, and 12 inches make
1 foot, how many feet are there in 4 metres? ....

Area and Perimeter

10 If the **perimeter** of a regular **hexagon** is
84 cm, what is the length of each side? ....

11 Mr Field wants to put a fence, made up of two strands of wire, around his paddock.
The paddock is a rectangle 55 m wide, and twice as long as it is wide.
There are two gates in the fence, each one is 3 m wide.
How many metres of wire does he need?

....

12 What is the length of a **rectangle** with a
perimeter of 26 cm and short sides of 2 cm? ....

13 What is the **area** of the shaded **triangle** below? .... ☐ 1

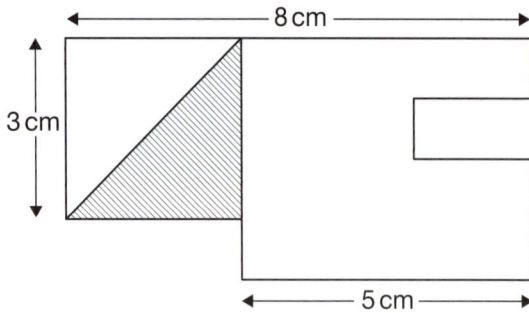

TOP TIP!

The area of a rectangle is length × width, and the area of a triangle is width × height ÷ 2. The answer should be in square units e.g. 2cm^2 or 8m^2

14 A **rectangle** is 25 cm long and has an **area** of 75 square cm. What is its width?

.... ☐ 1

Volume

15 What is the **volume** of a 10 cm cube?

....

TOP TIP!

The volume of a cuboid is length × width × height, and the answer should be in cubic units

16 How many centimetre cubes will fit into a box measuring 10 cm × 4 cm × 8 cm?

....

cubic centimetre 1cm^3
$1 \times 1 \times 1 \text{cm}^3$

☐ 1

☐ 1

☐ 1

17 How many **cubic centimetres** fit into a **cubic metre?**

....

☐ 1

18 The following 3D shape is made up of cm cubes. What is its volume?

....

☐ 1

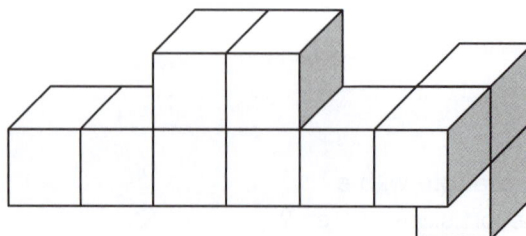

Time

19 17 minutes after 15:47 hours is ....

20 Use the following timetable to answer the questions below.

	1st train	2nd train	3rd train
Station A	10:16	10:40	11:04
Station B	10:35	?	11:23
Station C	10:54	11:18	?
Station D	11:06	11:30	11:50

The 1st and the 2nd trains take the same amount of time between each station.

a At what time will the 2nd train arrive at Station B? ....

b The 3rd train does not stop at Station C.
How much time is saved by catching the 3rd train rather than the 1st or 2nd train?

....

c There is a delay of 17 minutes at Station B one morning.

If the train is able to make up 4 minutes
between Station C and Station D, at what
time will the 2nd train now arrive at Station D? ....

21 Express 310.5 minutes as hours, minutes and seconds.

.... hours .... minutes .... seconds

22

	Bus A	Bus B	Bus C
Station	08:20	08:30	09:30
Garage	-	08:37	09:37
School	08:32	08:45	-
Park	08:40	08:58	09:48
Supermarket	08:52	09:09	10:00

Which bus has the quickest journey from the station to the park? ....

NVR Complete the Pair

WORKED EXAMPLE

Which shape or pattern completes the second pair in the same way as the first pair? Underline the answer.

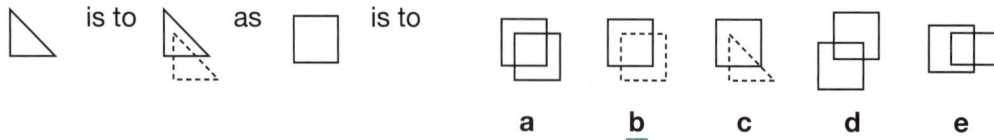

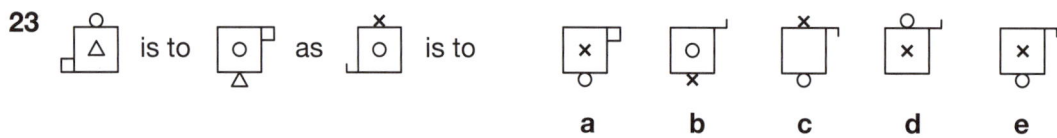

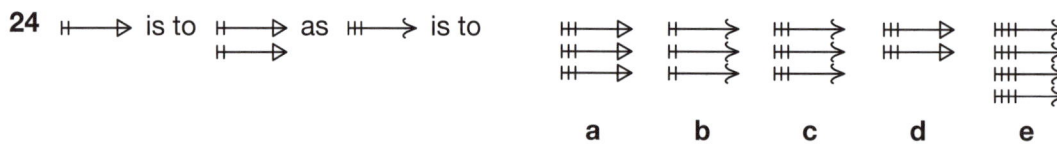

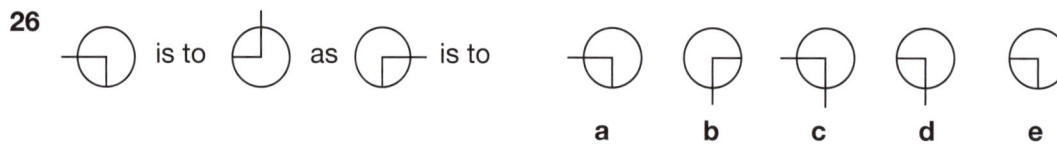

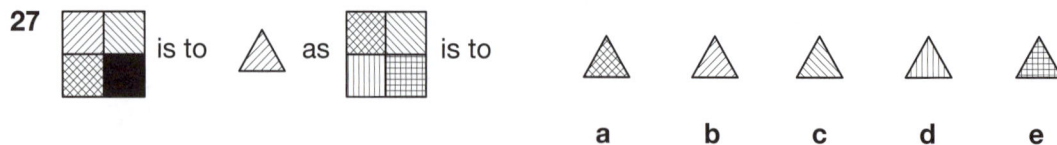

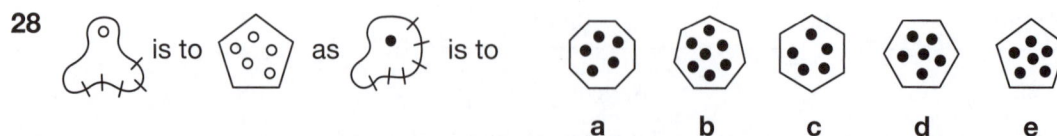

In the first pair, the second pattern has an additional triangle with a dotted outline. Answer b has two squares, with one with a dotted outline, so this completes the second pair in the same way as the first.

Which shape or pattern completes the second pair in the same way as the first pair? Underline the answer.

23

24

25

26

27

28

6

Total
37

Statistics

KEY SKILL

Graphs are used to show sets of data

- When reading data from a graph always check the scale along each axis of the graph. The x axis is along the bottom of the graph and the y axis is up the side of the graph

- Whatever scale is used it must be used consistently along the axis, e.g. the axes may increase by 5 or 10 each time

- In a line graph, the points where the x and y axes meet on the graph give the value and a line is drawn to link them

- In a bar graph it is the height or length of the bar that indicates value, with each bar representing a different category

- If the data is being represented in a pictogram, check the key to find out what each symbol represents

- A tally chart is a simple way of counting and recording amounts. Remember that the 'lines' used are grouped in fives – four lines with the fifth one crossing through them ⅢⅠ

30 mins

Bar Charts

1   The bar graph shows the number of newspapers sold each day for a week.

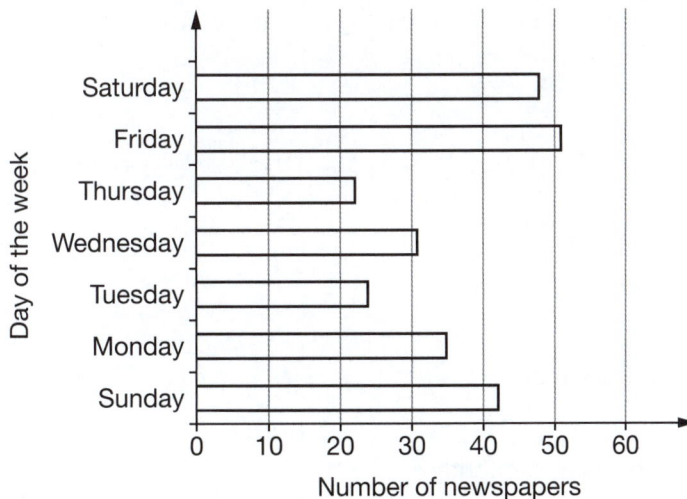

a How many more newspapers were sold on Sunday than Thursday? ....

b How many papers were sold altogether on Friday, Saturday and Sunday? ....

c If Tuesday's sales increase by 25% next week, how many papers will be sold on Tuesday? 3

2 The frequency of the five vowels 'a','e','i','o' and 'u' in a piece of writing was recorded using a tally chart.

Here are the results.

a	卌 卌 卌 卌 卌 卌 卌 卌 卌
e	卌 卌 卌 卌 卌 卌 卌 卌 卌 卌 卌 卌 卌
i	卌 卌 卌 卌 卌 卌 卌 卌 卌 卌
o	卌 卌 卌 卌 卌 卌 卌
u	卌 卌 卌 卌

a Show this data on the bar chart below: 2

Frequency (y-axis: 0, 10, 20, 30, 40, 50, 60)

Vowels (x-axis: a, e, i, o, u)

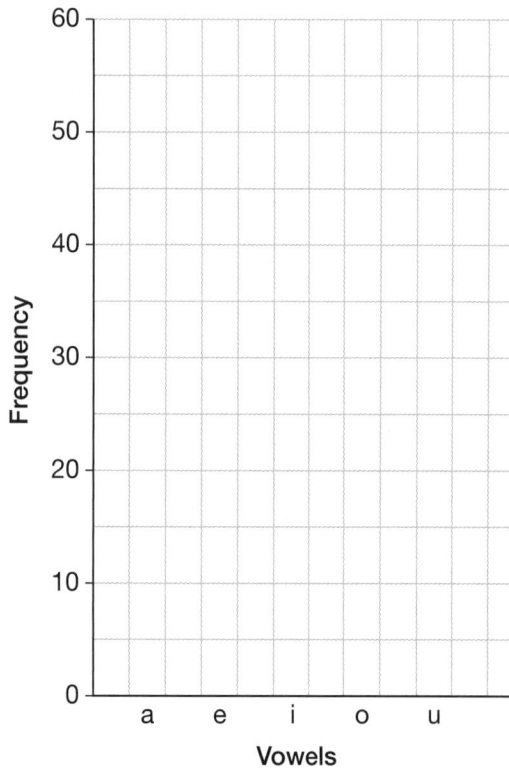

b Which vowel was least common? ....

c Which vowel was used most frequently? ....

d On how many occasions were vowels used in the piece of writing? ....

e What percentage of the vowels were 'u'? 4

44

Line Graphs

3 Naveen measured the temperature each hour and plotted it on a line graph.

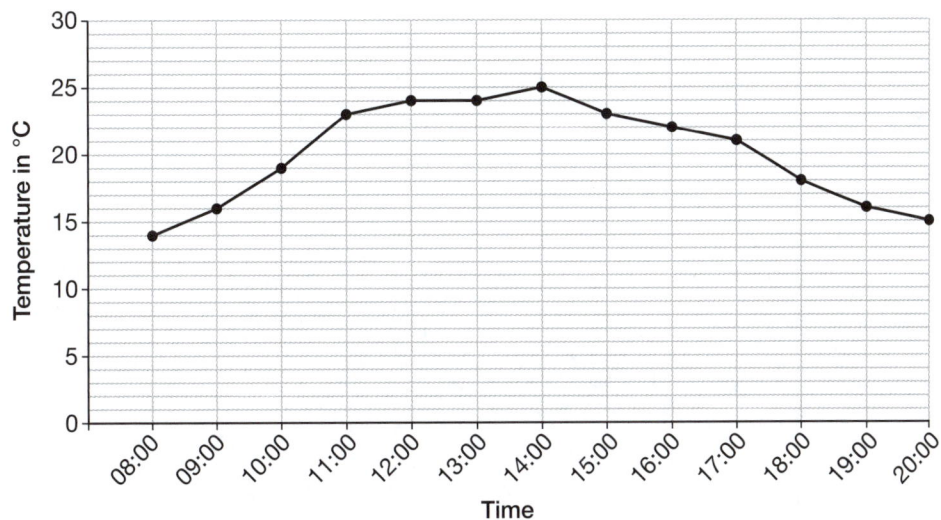

a What was the temperature at midday?

....

TOP TIP!

When reading a value from a line graph, use a pencil or ruler to follow the grid lines accurately

b By how much did the temperature drop between 16:00 and 20:00?

....

c For approximately how many hours was the temperature above 20°C ....

4 This graph shows the temperature measured on 8 occasions every hour from 9.00a.m.

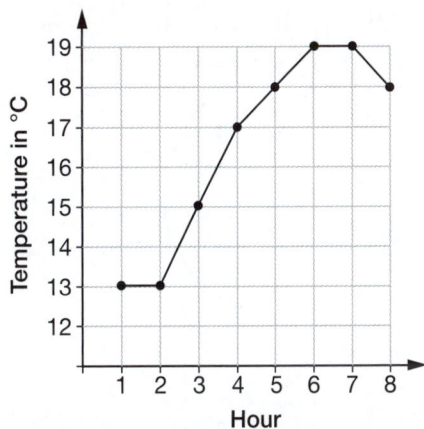

At 9.00a.m. it was 13°C.

a By how many degrees did the temperature rise between 9.00a.m. and 12.00 noon? ....

b From the graph estimate the temperature at 11.30a.m. ....

c Which was the hottest hour during the time recorded? .... 3 ☐

Venn Diagrams

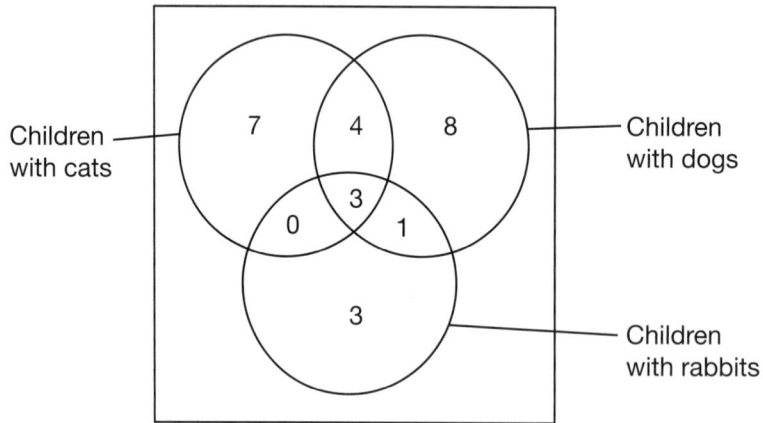

5 a How many children in the class have both a dog and a cat? ....

b If there are 30 children in the class, how
many do not have a cat or a dog or a rabbit? .... 2 ☐

6 Of the three chosen pizza toppings shown in the diagram, which one is the most
popular?

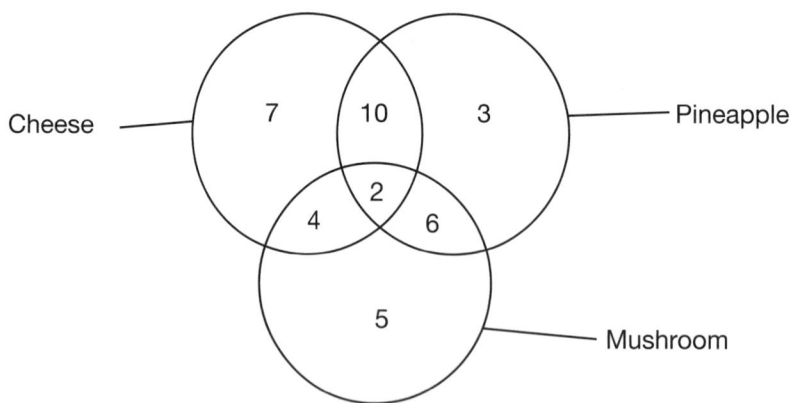

.... 1 ☐

Tables

Temp in °C	Jan	Feb	Mar	Apr	May	Jun	Jul	Aug	Sep	Oct	Nov	Dec
Min	−6	−4	2	6	9	10	10	9	6	3	3	−2
Max	8	9	12	17	21	24	26	27	25	21	16	10

Use this data to answer the next three questions.

7   Which month has the greatest difference between
its average minimum and average maximum temperature?   1

8   How many months have an average
maximum temperature greater than 12 degrees?   1

9   Between which two successive months is the
difference in maximum temperatures the greatest?   1

Pictograms

10 How many more pupils play hockey than tennis?

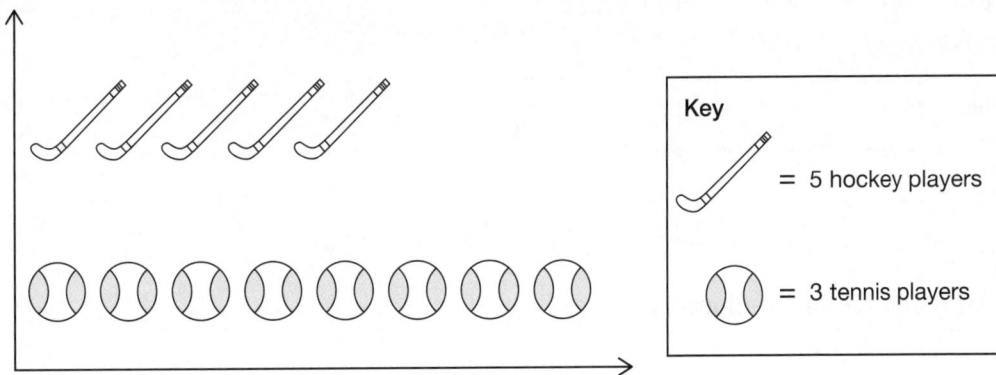

Key

= 5 hockey players

= 3 tennis players

....   1

Total
22

Curveball Questions 1

KEY SKILL

In many maths and non-verbal reasoning questions a key skill is to work carefully and systematically through the information given, whether it is in diagrams, numbers or words.

To solve the problem, you should only use the information given, not any general knowledge that you might have!

Logic

When trying to solve a problem where the information is written in sentences, it can help to make a table or diagram setting out what you are given, and expressing the information in simple equations. For example:

Tom is 3 years younger than his sister Jodie. Jodie is one-third of her mother's age and twice as old as her youngest brother Sam. If Jodie's mother is 39, how old are Tom and Sam?

Sam	Tom	Jodie	Mother
$S = J \div 2$	$T = J - 3$	$J = 2S$	$M = 42$
		$J = M \div 3$	

We can find J by substituting: $J = M \div 3 = 42 \div 3 = 14$

Then substitute further: $T = 14 - 3 = 11$ and $S = 14 \div 2 = 7$; so Tom is 11 and Sam is 7.

⏱ 30 mins

1 Lions eat meat. Lions are mammals.

If the two statements above are true, underline the statement below that must also be true.

All mammals eat meat.   Some mammals eat meat.

Some lions are mammals.   All mammals are lions.

1

2 One-third of a bag of counters is green.

There are 20 green counters and just one yellow counter in the bag.

If the remaining counters are red and blue, and there are twice as many red as blue, how many blue counters are there?

[3]

3 From the codes given below match the word to the correct code:

A = 1, D = 5, E = 3, R = 4, S = 7, T = 9

94153   79143   51937   93173

DATES   TEASE   STARE   TRADE

[2]

4 Complete these number grids to make the numbers in each row and in each column add up to the total given below the grid.

a

5		3
		4
1		

15

b

	10	
		8
8	5	

20

c

	6	
3		
	15	2

25

d

14		
	13	
	10	8

30

[10]

Total
16

Mixed Paper 1

40 mins

Logic and Sequences

1 What number comes next in these sequences?

a 26, 27, 29, 32, 36, ...

c 1004, 1105, 1206, 1307, ...

b 65, 52, 39, 26, ...

d 1, 4, 16, 64, ...

2

2 Three children go to the zoo. Tickets are £10.50 for adults and half price for children.

How much do they have for drinks after buying their tickets, if they have a £20 note between them?

....

2

> **TOP TIP!**
>
> If there are two marks for a problem question, show each step of your calculation

Which picture or pattern on the bottom row comes next in the pattern on the top row? Underline the answer.

> **TOP TIP!**
>
> When multiple options are given it may help to cross out answers as you eliminate them

3

4

5

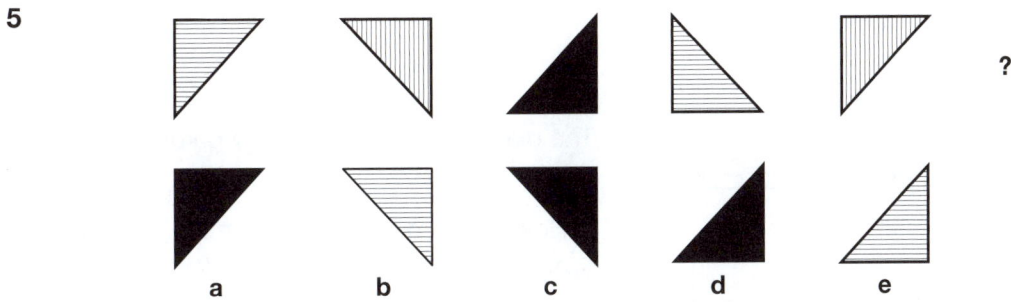

6

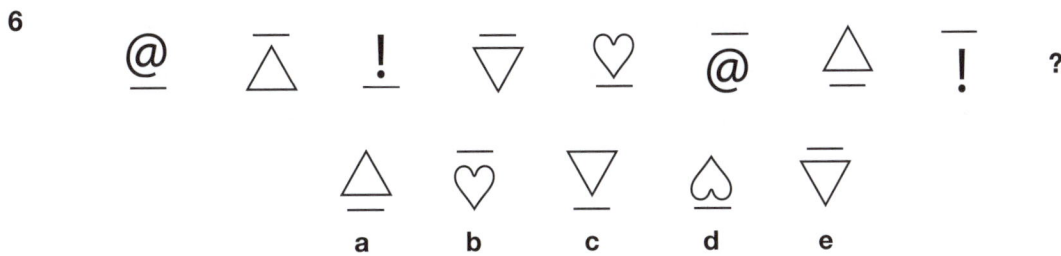

7

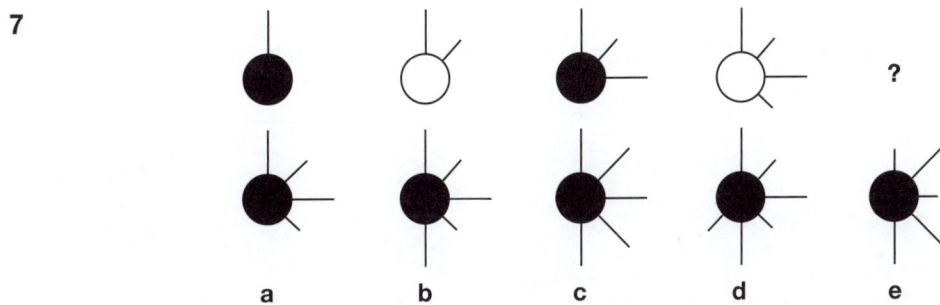

8 Mrs Brown has three children. The eldest is 5 years older than the youngest.

The middle child is 2 years younger than the eldest, and 25 years younger than Mrs Brown.

If Mrs Brown is 37 years old, what is the age of her youngest child? ....

Number Skills

9 At the school sports day Ben, Saqif, Doug and Ali all enter the sprint.

Saqif is faster than Doug but 7 seconds behind Ali.

Ben has a time of 47 seconds.

Doug is 10 seconds behind Ali who is 2 seconds behind Ben.

> **TOP TIP!**
>
> Remember: In questions on races, the quickest time is the shortest time!

If Doug's time is 59 seconds, what was Saqif's time? ....

5

2

3

10 Underline the odd one out: $\frac{3}{10}$ 30%   30 $\frac{9}{30}$ $\frac{6}{9}$ 300.3

1

11 4.2 m + 33 cm + 16 mm = ... cm

1

12

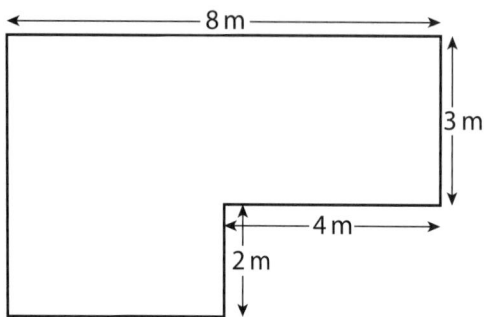

The diagram gives a plan of a garden.

a How many metres of fencing are needed to go round the edge?

....

b If a quarter of the garden is made into a patio, what is the **area** of the patio?

....

2

8 m — 3 m — 4 m — 2 m

Statistics

13 This bar graph shows the percentage of pupils in a class with each type of pet.

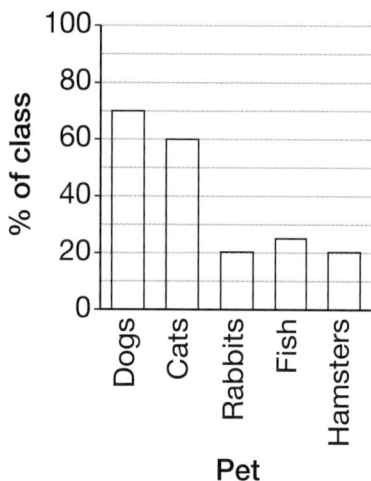

% of class

100
80
60
40
20
0

Dogs   Cats   Rabbits   Fish   Hamsters

Pet

a What percentage had rabbits? ....

b If there were 20 children in the class, how many children had cats? ....

c If half of those who had dogs also had cats, how many children had cats and dogs?

....

d How many more children had fish than hamsters? ....

4

Special Numbers and Place Value

14 53 721.046

Add together the digit in the tens column and the digit in the hundredths column.

.... [1]

15 Underline the **prime** numbers: [1]

3   8   10   13   29   42

16 What is the value of five cubed? .... [1]

17 Half of a jar of sweets are red, a quarter are yellow and one-fifth are green, the rest are orange. If there are 80 sweets in the jar how many are orange?

.... [1]

18 $(4 \times 6) + (69 - 14) =$ .... [1]

19 $584 - (45 \times 3) =$ .... [1]

20 $(5^2 + 6^2) + (217 \div 7) =$ .... [1]

> **TOP TIP!**
>
> **Work out the brackets and indices first**

21 A litre of drink contains 400 ml of orange juice and 25 ml of lemon juice, made up to 1 litre with soda water. How many ml of soda water are needed to make 2 litres of the drink?

.... [1]

22 What is the volume in cubic metres of a crate that is 1 m long, 50 cm wide and 80 cm high? Give your answer in centimetres.

.... [1]

23 What is the code for the pattern on the right? .... [1]

AS   BT   AT   CR   ?

24 Which shape on the left does not belong to the set on the right?

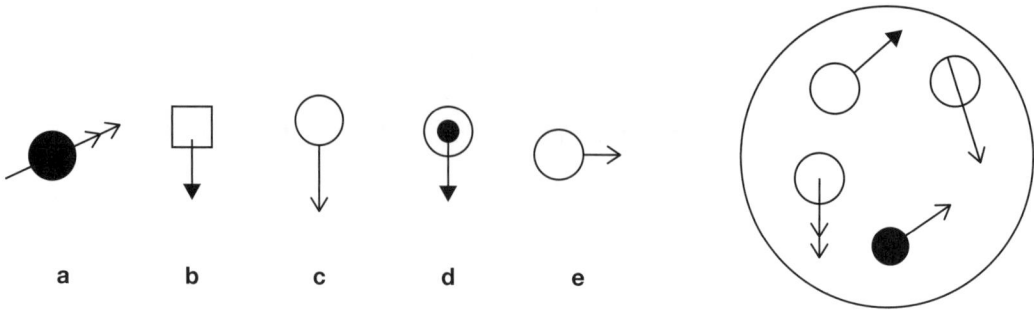

a   b   c   d   e

....

25 Which pattern on the right is a reflection of the pattern on the left?

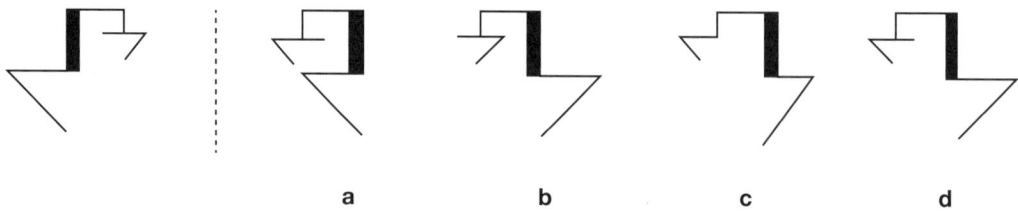

a   b   c   d

Shape, Space and Nets

26 Three of the internal angles of a quadrilateral are 57°, 85° and 120°.

What is the size of the fourth angle? ....

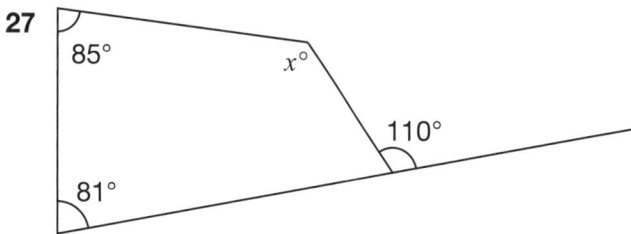

27

85° $x°$

110°

81°

Angle x = ...

28 Which net on the left will fold to give the cube on the right? Underline the answer.

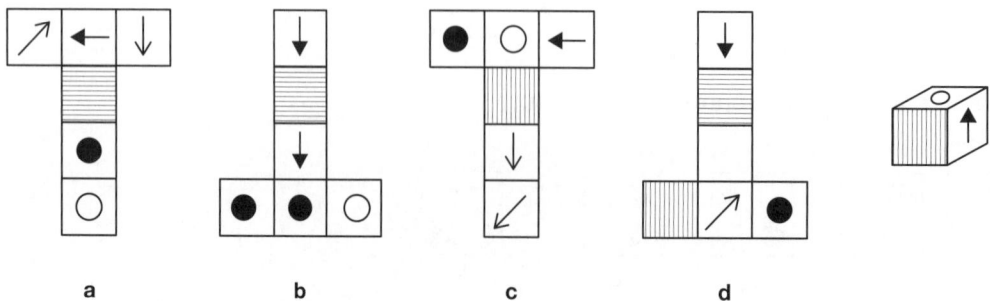

a   b   c   d

Coordinates

29

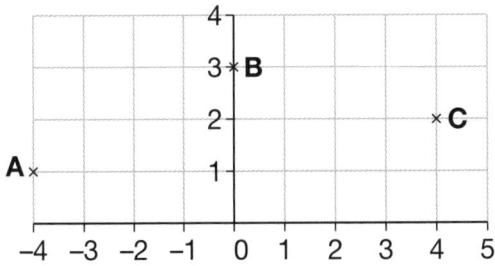

Give the coordinates of the following points:

A = ...   B = ...   C = ...   `1`

30 Plot and join the following points. What type of triangle is formed?

(3,4)   (3,7)   (7,2)

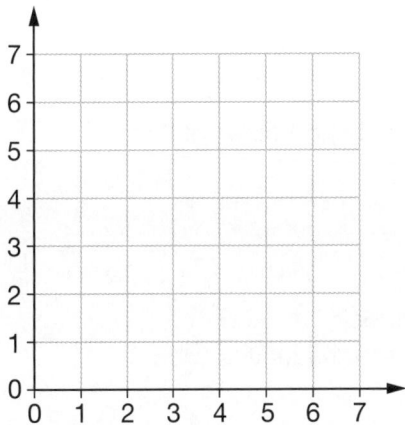

....   `2`

31 Reflect the triangle ABC in the *y* axis and label it A, B, C. Give the coordinates of the new triangle.

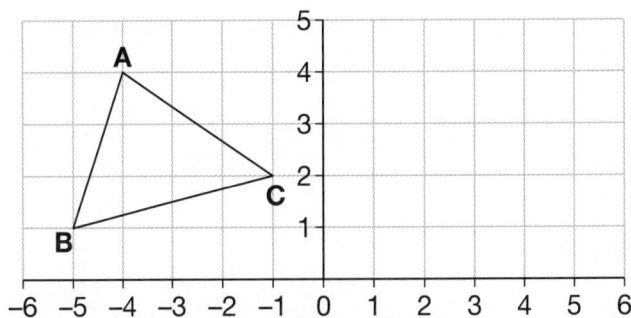

> **TOP TIP!**
>
> **Here the *y* axis is acting as the mirror line or line of reflection**

A = ...   B = ...   C = ...   `1`

Total
40

Mixed Paper 2

40 mins

1 Underline the odd one out.

25   81   144   36   24

1

2 67 + 22 = 100 − ....

1

3 Give 4 **factors** for each of the following numbers:

a 35 ....

b 20 ....

> **factor** A number that divides exactly into another number, with no remainder

c 33 ....

3

4 What is the length of a rectangle with **perimeter** 26 cm and short sides of 2 cm?

....

1

5 A farmer wants to put one strand of wire around his paddock.
The paddock is a rectangle 80 m wide, and three times as long as it is wide.
There are three gates in the fence, each one 3 m wide.
How many metres of wire does he need?

....

1

6 A fruit drink is made up of 20% cordial, 20% orange, 20% pineapple and the rest is lemonade. Tilly uses 2 litres of lemonade.

a How much fruit drink is made all together? ....litres

b How many 200 ml glasses can be filled? ....

2

7 Ice creams are £1.20 each, lollies are 80p and chocolate bars are 99p.

What is the change from a £20 note after buying 3 of each? ....

3

Which shape or pattern on the right belongs to the group on the left? Underline the answer.

Example

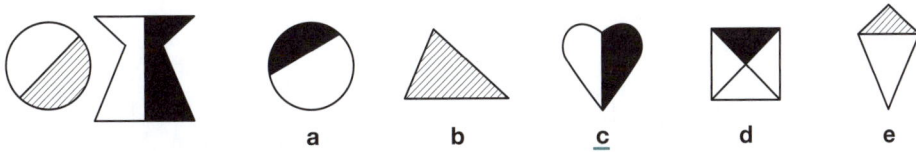

a   b   <u>c</u>   d   e

TOP TIP!

Look carefully at the shapes on the left and identify things that are common to them all

8

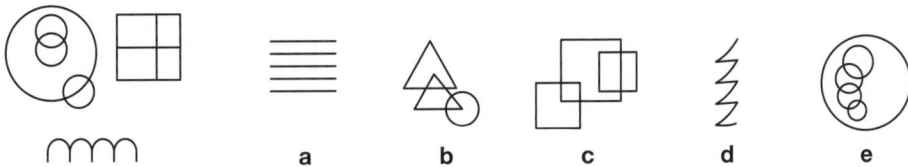

a   b   c   d   e

9

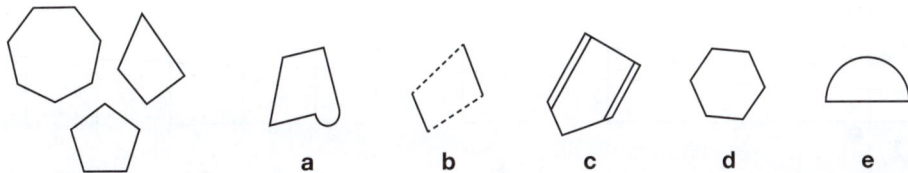

a   b   c   d   e

10

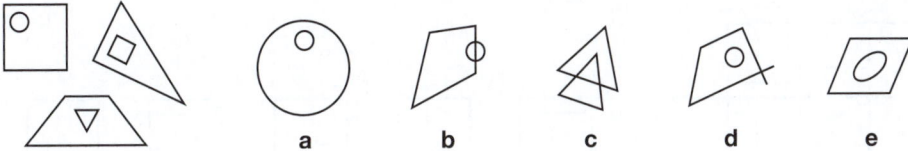

a   b   c   d   e

11

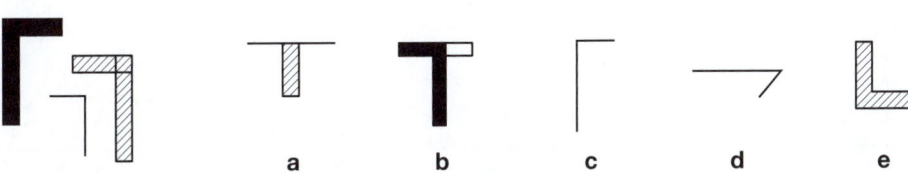

a   b   c   d   e

12

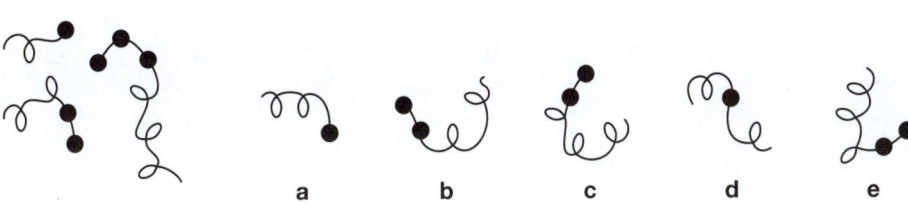

a   b   c   d   e

5

Which pattern completes the larger shape or grid? Underline the answer.

Example

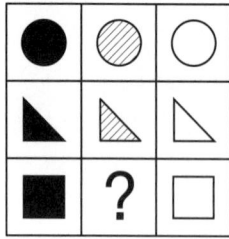

a   <u>b</u>   c   d   e

13

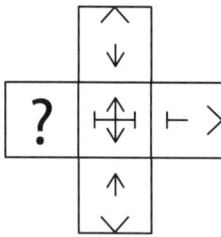

a   b   c   d   e

14

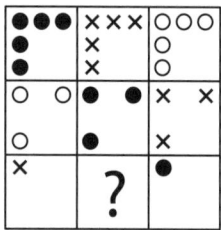

a   b   c   d   e

15

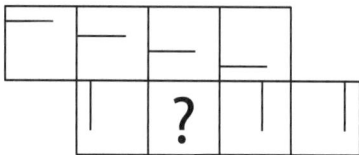

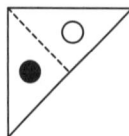 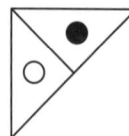 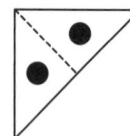 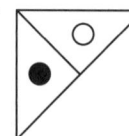 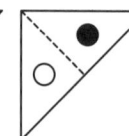

a   b   c   d   e

16

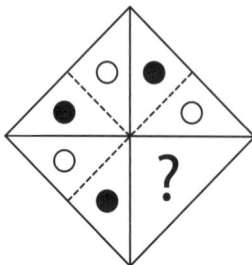

a   b   c   d   e

4

17 Look at this plan of a field:

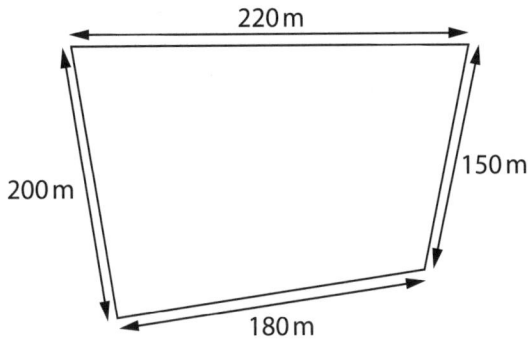

a What is the **perimeter**? ....

b How many circuits around the field must a runner do to cover 3 km, assuming the

runner goes along the perimeter line? ....

2

18 A candle burns at the rate of 3 cm every hour. A 15 cm candle is lit at 7.30 p.m

How tall will the candle be at 10 minutes past 10 that evening? ....

2

19 Some children were taking the temperature of hot water every minute and the results were plotted on a graph. The water was at 100°C at 1 minute, then left to cool.

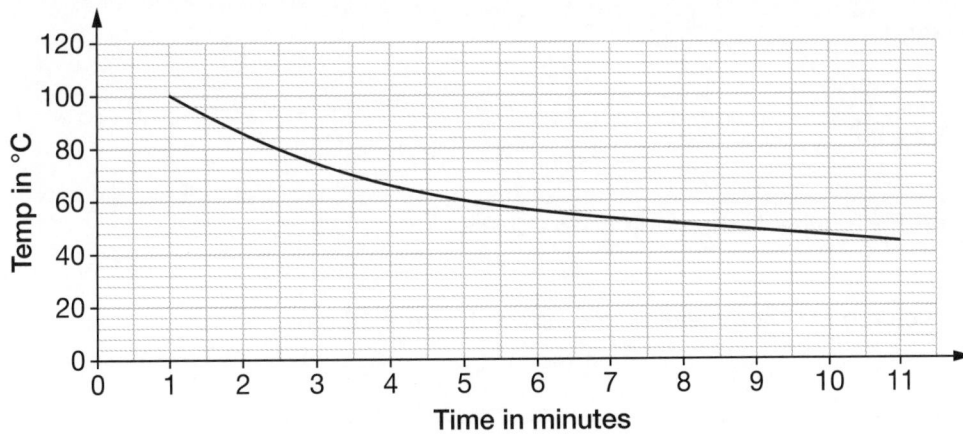

a What was the temperature after 11 minutes? ....

b Approximately how long did it take for the temperature to drop from 100°C to 80°C?

....

2

20 **Round** 638.87 to:

a the nearest tenth ....

b the nearest whole number ....

c the nearest hundred. ....

1

21 **a** Give six **factors** of 60 excluding 1 and 60 ....

b Underline the numbers that are multiples of 7:

35   47   54   63   81

c Give a **factor** of 16 and a **multiple** less than 50 of 16.

Factor .... Multiple ....

3

22 A survey found that two thirds of all train journeys arrived within five minutes of their scheduled time. Twenty-four, or one-quarter, of all trains were exactly on time. How many arrived within five minutes of their scheduled time?

....

1

23 **a** $3x + 17 = 35$ $x =$ ....

b $640 \div 4 = y + 60$ $y =$ ....

c If $a = 3$ and $b = 8$, what is the value of $4b - 2a$? ....

3

24 What is the **volume** of a box measuring 40 cm × 12 cm × 10 cm?

....

1

25 How many faces are there on an octagonal prism?

....

1

26 Which net on the right can be folded to give the cube on the left?

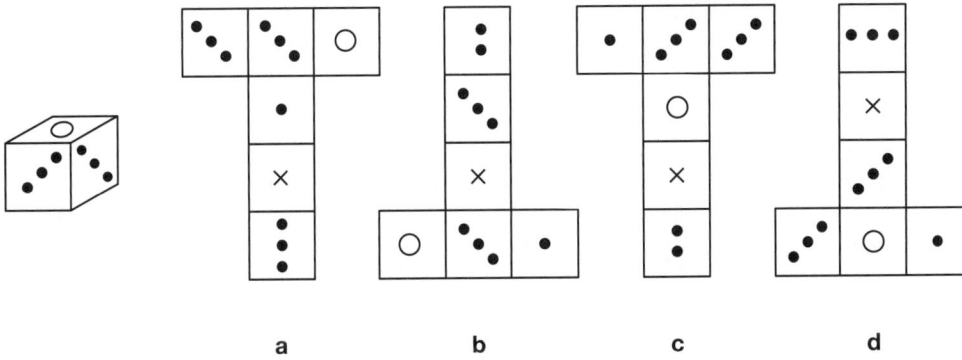

a   b   c   d

1

27 The triangle P, Q, R is translated by 4 across and 2 up, to give P' Q' R'.

Draw P' Q' R' on the graph below.

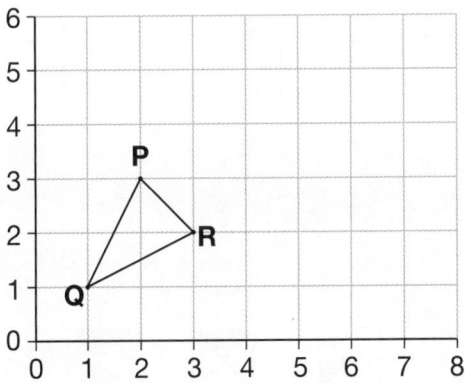

1

28 What is the code for the pattern on the right?

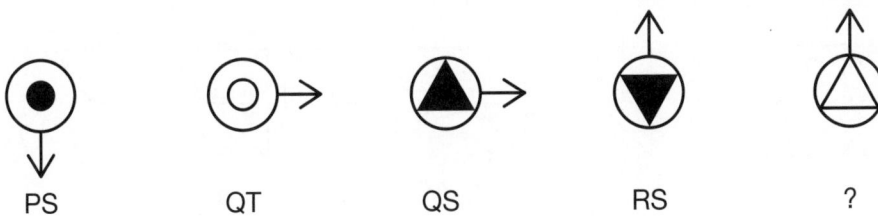

PS   QT   QS   RS   ?

1

Total
40

Mixed Paper 3

Which pattern completes the larger shape or grid? Underline the answer.

Example

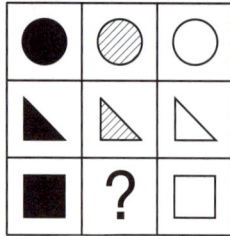

a   <u>b</u>   c   d   e

45 mins

1

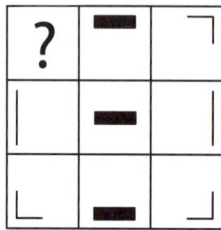

a   b   c   d   e

2

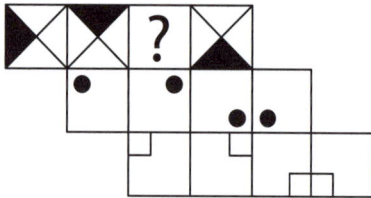

a   b   c   d   e

3

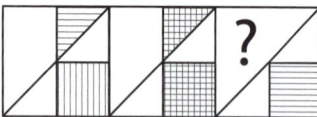

a   b   c   d   e

4

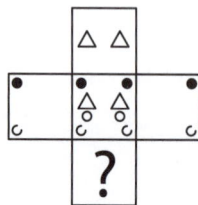

a   b   c   d   e

4

Which pattern on the right is a reflection of the pattern on the left? Underline the answer.

Example

a   b   <u>c</u>   d   e

5

a   b   c   d   e

6

a   b   c   d   e

7

a   b   c   d   e

8

a   b   c   d   e

4

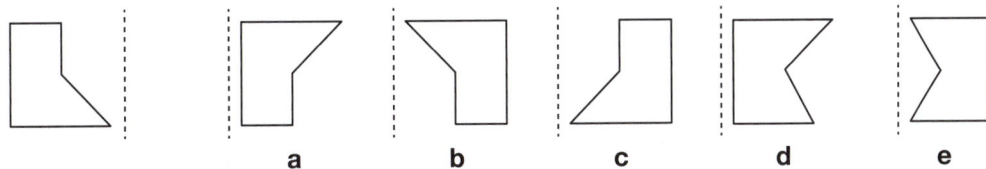

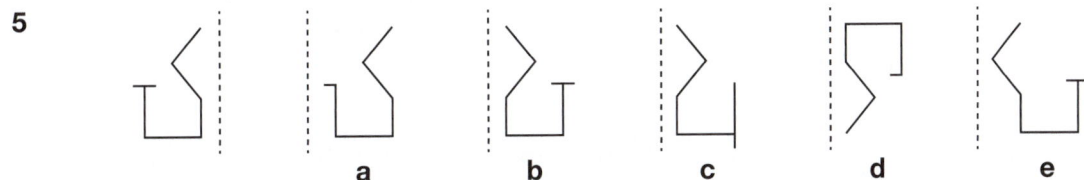

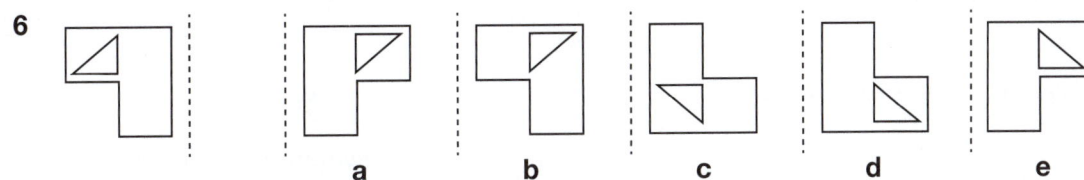

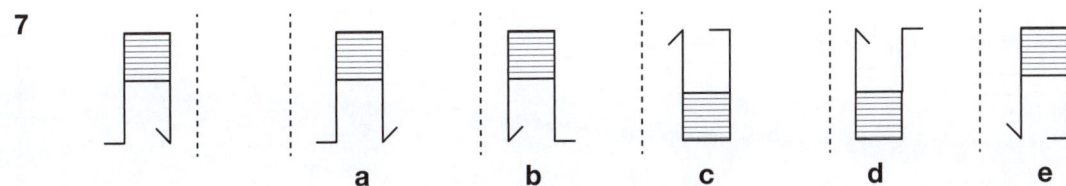

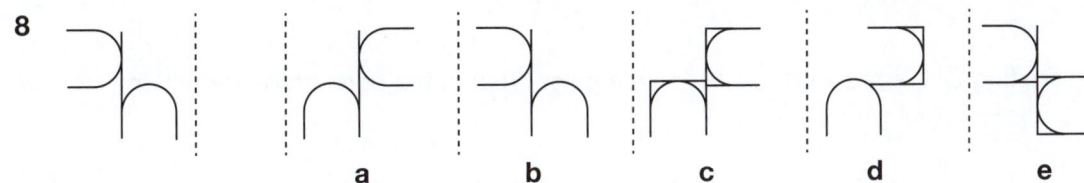

9 From the number 6 420 135.7 write in words the value of:

> **TOP TIP!**
>
> **Look at the column in which the digit is placed to find out its value**

a the digit 4 ....

b the digit 7 ....

1

10 **Round** the following numbers to the nearest 10:

a 769.8.......................   **b** 990.59 ....

1

11 403 + 72 + 3023 = ...

12 What number is 471 less than 2000? ....

13 $12^2 - 6^2$ = ...

14 What is the sum of $3^3 + 5^3 - 1^3$ = ...

15 Which number comes next?

    a 4, 12, 20, 28, ...   **b** 78, 71, 64, 57, ...

    c 10 970, 10 980, 10 990, ...

16 Underline the equivalent fractions:

$$\frac{4}{6} \qquad \frac{9}{10} \qquad \frac{5}{15} \qquad \frac{16}{24} \qquad \frac{3}{15} \qquad \frac{1}{6}$$

17 Reduce the following fractions to their simplest form:

    a $\frac{5}{25}$ = ...   **b** $\frac{6}{9}$ = ...   **c** $\frac{14}{16}$ = ...

18 15% of £500 = ...

19 A bag costing £24 is reduced to £19.20 in a sale. What is the percentage reduction?

....

20 73 + 6x = 145, x = ...

21 If a = 10 and b = 13, what is the value of $a^2 - 3b$? ....

22 If the diameter of a circle is 5.8 cm, what is its radius?

....

23 How many vertices are there on an octagonal based pyramid?

....

24 Plot and label the following coordinates on the grid below:

X (−2,3)   Y (1,3)   Z (3,2)

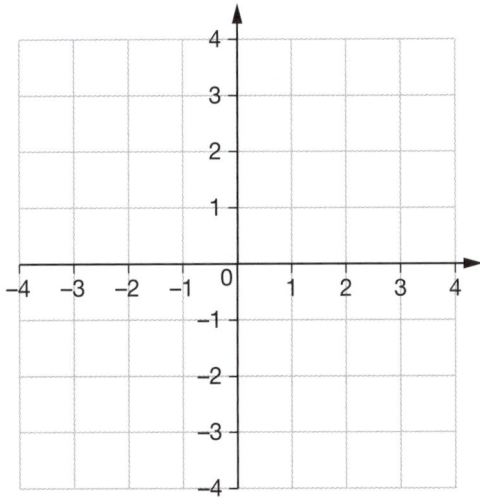

25 The coordinates of a ship on a grid were (3,−5). If the
ship moves 7 squares north, what are its new coordinates? ....

26 Convert 745 mm to metres ....

27 Convert five and a quarter kilograms to grams. ....

28 What is the volume of a wooden chest measuring 1.5 m × 50 cm × 80 cm?
Underline the correct answer.

a 12 m³

b 6 000 000 cm³

c 6000 cm³

d 6.5 m³

e 60 000 cm³

> **TOP TIP!**
>
> Check the units and the
> number of zeros very carefully

29 How many cartons of 450 ml can be filled from a catering container of 90 litres?

....

30 A count was made of all the vowels occurring in a piece of writing and the results were shown on a bar graph.

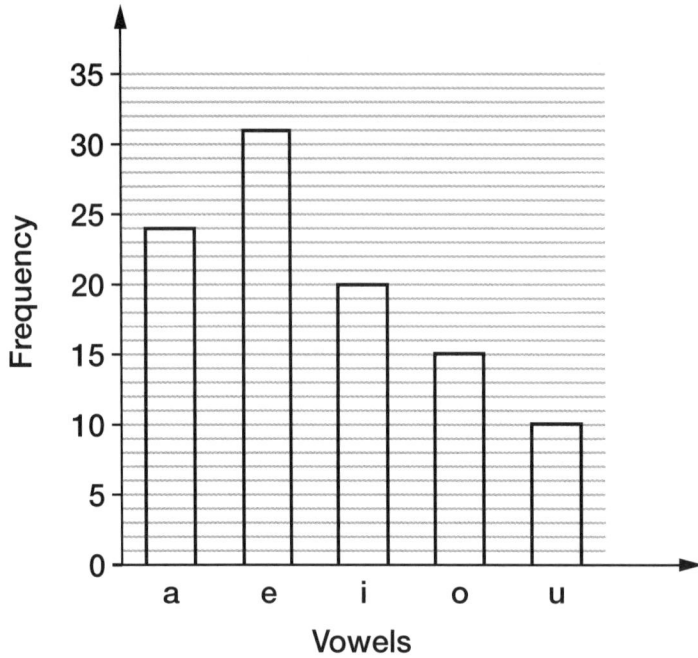

a How many more times was 'e' recorded than 'u'? ....

b What fraction of the vowels recorded were 'i'? ....

c The name Ellie occurred 5 times in the piece of writing. If the name was changed to Ann, what would the new totals be for each vowel?

a ....

e ....

i ....

o ....

u ....

5

31 The pictogram shows the weather for two weeks.

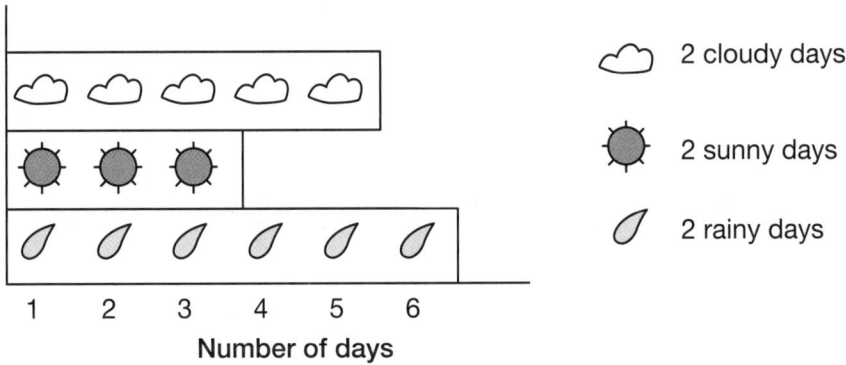

☁ 2 cloudy days

☀ 2 sunny days

◊ 2 rainy days

Number of days

How many more days were rainy than sunny? .... ☐ 1

32 Using the information below, complete the pictogram to show the favourite fruits of a class of 24 children.

Number of children selecting favourite fruits:

Oranges 5   Bananas 4   Apples 8   Grapes 7

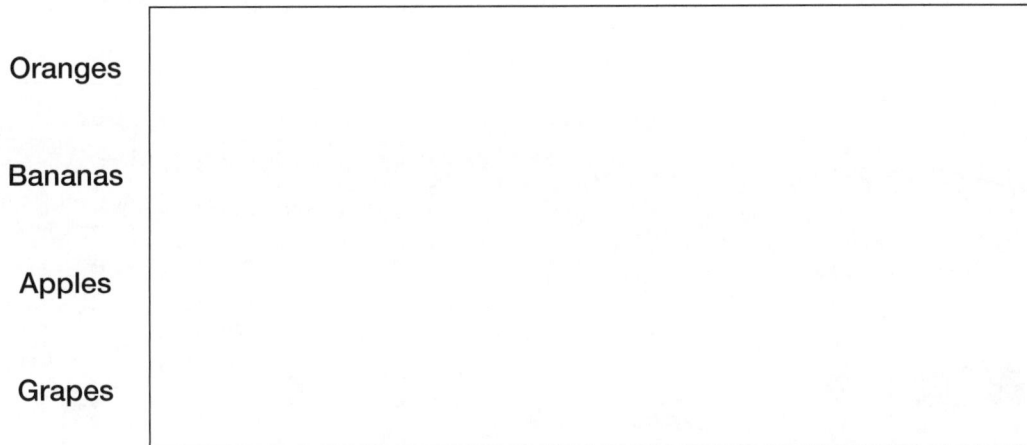

Oranges

Bananas

Apples

Grapes

Key   One picture represents one child's choice

☐ 1

33 Calculate the size of angles *a* and *b*.

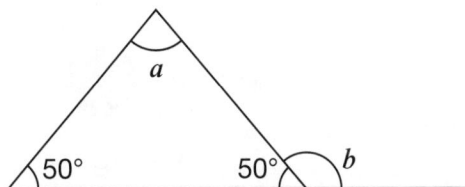

a = ...

b = ...

☐ 1

34 An ice skater spins two-and-a-quarter turns, through how many degrees does he spin? .... ☐ 1

Total
40

Mixed Paper 4

Which shape or pattern on the right belongs to the group on the left?
Underline the answer.

Example

a   b   c   d   e

40 mins

1

a   b   c   d   e

2

a   b   c   d   e

3

a   b   c   d   e

4

a   b   c   d   e

4

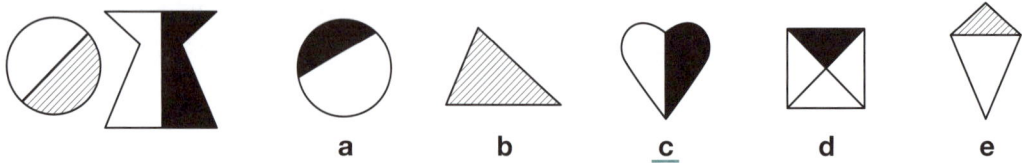

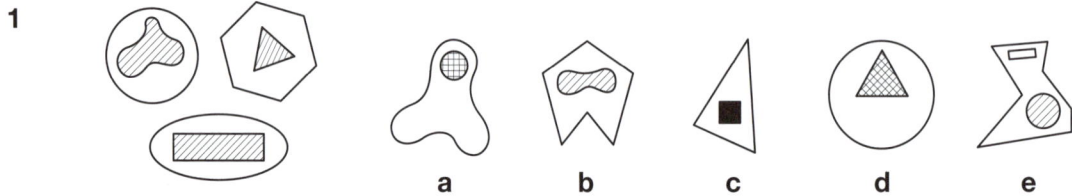

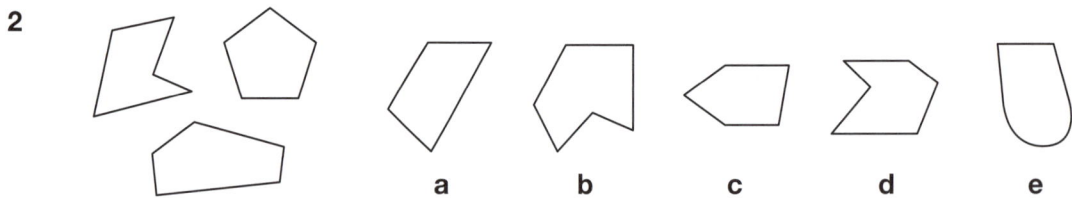

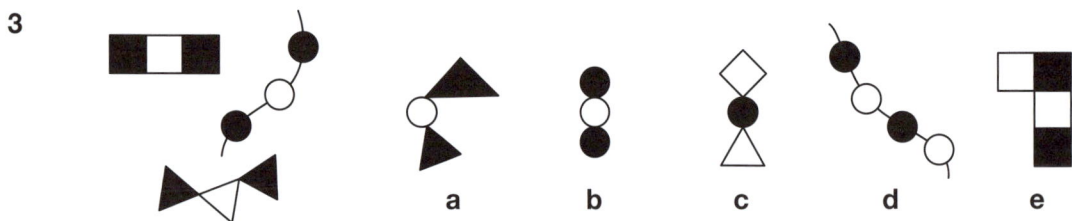

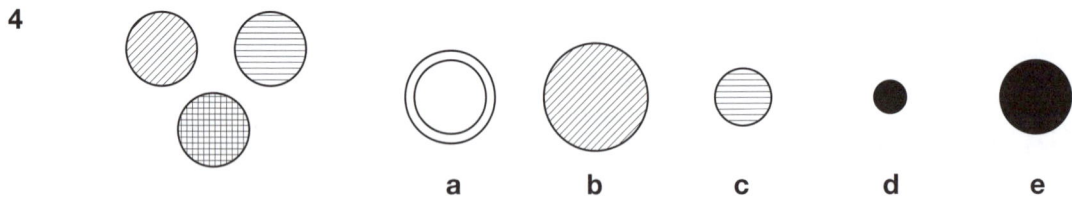

5 Write the number thirteen million, thirteen thousand and thirteen in digits.

....

1

6 Add the digit in the hundreds column
to the digit in the hundredths column.   4702.483 .... `1`

7 What is the total of 106 and 45 and 29.5? .... `1`

8 56 less than 409 is .... `1`

9 Give 4 factors of 100, excluding 1 and 100. .... `1`

10 Give three multiples of 17 which are less than 100 .... `1`

TOP TIP!

Matching nets to cubes can be tricky. Cut out a net from rough paper and fold it to help you learn which faces will meet and which edges are shared

In questions 11–14, which of the nets on the left will fold to give the cube on the right?

11

a   b   c   d

12

a   b   c   d

13

a   b   c   d   e

14

a   b   c   d   e

`4`

15 Complete these triplets so that they each make a total of 1000:

    a 790   140   ?   ....

    b 499   392   ?   ....

    c 67   10   ?   .... `3`

16 In a race, Kelly is faster than Jen but 5 seconds slower than Annie. Annie was 11 seconds ahead of Jen. How many seconds was Jen behind Kelly? .... `2`

17 In a car rally, the red car is quicker than the blue car but slower than the grey and green ones. The yellow car is faster than the green car.

    If the grey car is slower than the green car, which car came first? .... `2`

18 In a jar of 250 sweets, half are cherry, one-fifth are lemon and a tenth are lime. The rest are orange.

    a What percentage are orange? ....

    b How many are orange? .... `2`

19 $10^2 - (3 \times 6) + (48 \div 6) =$ .... `1`

20 $3^3 - 2^3 + (39 \div 3) =$ .... `1`

21 Give the value of the angles labelled x and y in the diagram:

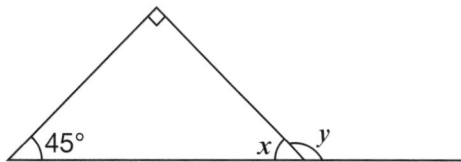

$x =$ ....

$y =$ .... `2`

22 What are the coordinates of the vertices of the quadrilateral PQRS?

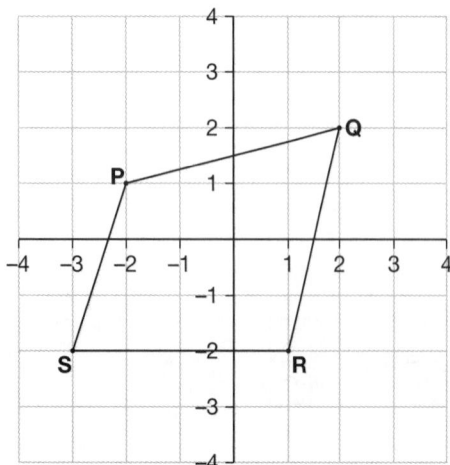

P = ...

Q = ...

R = ...

S = ... `2`

23 The diagram gives a plan of a garden.

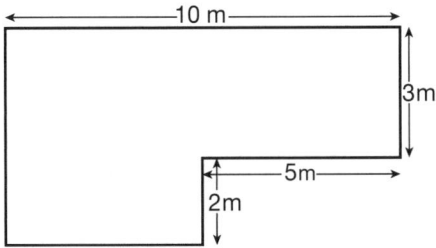

10 m
3 m
5 m
2 m

a How many metres of fencing are needed to go round the edge? ....

b If a quarter of the garden is made into a patio, what is the area of the patio?

....

2

24 The shape is made up of centimetre cubes. What is its total **volume**?

....

1

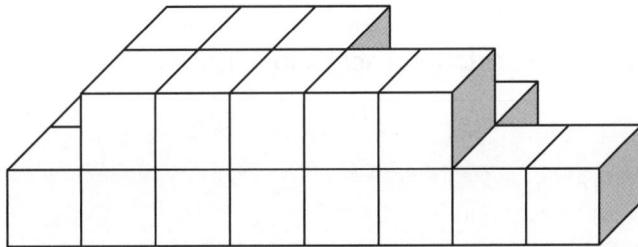

25 How much larger is the **volume** of box A than box B? ....

1

Box A measures 3 cm × 6 cm × 8 cm   Box B measures 4 cm × 5 cm × 6 cm

26

Urdu speakers
9
1
6
Mandarin speakers
7
4
5
10
Spanish speakers

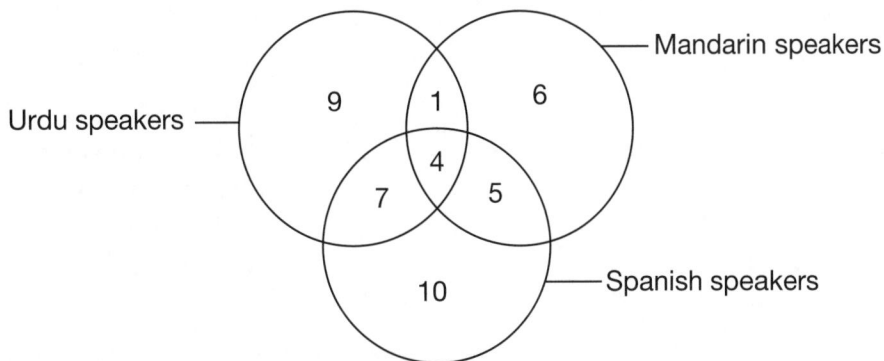

a How many people speak mandarin? ....

b How many people speak two languages? ....

2

27

Small Shirts	
Large Shirts	
Small T-shirts	
Large T-shirts	
Small Jumpers	
Large Jumpers	

Key

= 3	Small Shirts
= 3	Large Shirts
= 3	Small T-shirts
= 3	Large T-shirts
= 3	Small Jumpers
= 3	Large Jumpers

a How many more large T-shirts were sold than small jumpers? ....

b How many small and large shirts were sold altogether?   2

28 Express 82% as:

a a fraction in its lowest terms ....

b a decimal   1

29 Convert these fractions to decimals:

a $\dfrac{3}{4}$ ....

b $\dfrac{7}{20}$ 1

30 What is the total of $\dfrac{1}{2} + \dfrac{1}{4} + \dfrac{1}{8} =$ 1

TOP TIP!

Fractions need to have the same denominator in order to be added together

Total **40**

Finished these Mixed Papers? Go online at www.bond11plus.co.uk and register for FREE RESOURCES to get two additional Mixed Papers.

Curveball Questions 2

7 mins

Look carefully at the two patterns below, remembering to be systematic.

There are 18 differences between them. Find the differences in the patterns. Record the squares where the differences occur by giving the letter from the *x* axis and the number from the *y* axis.

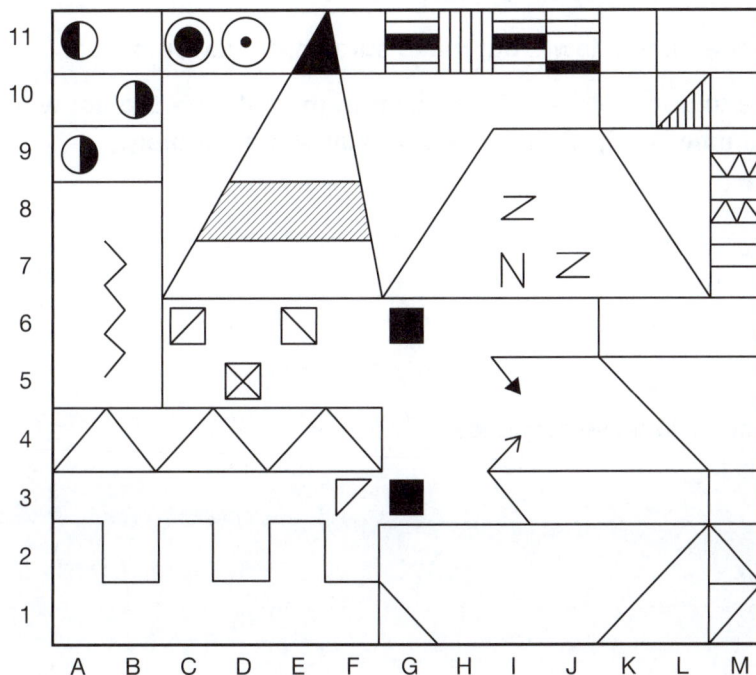

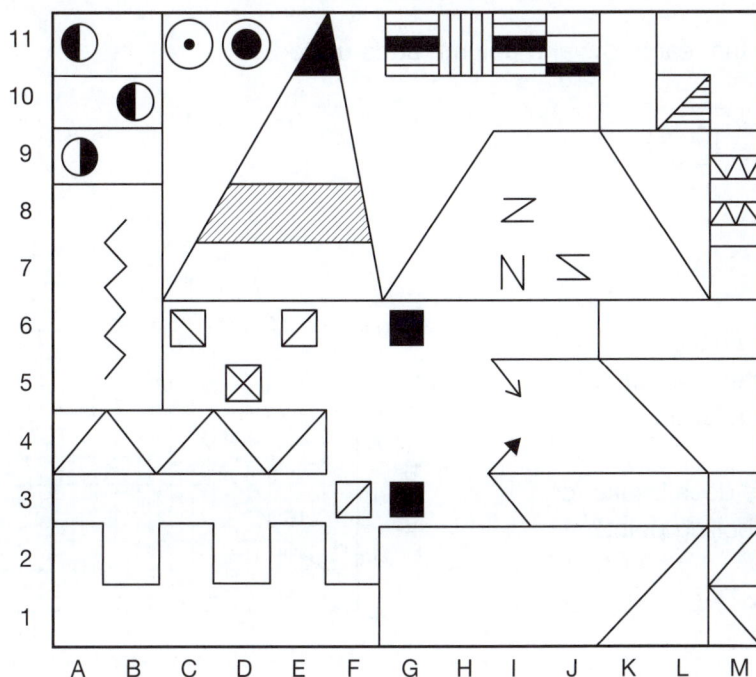

Test Paper 1

TOP TIP!

- Do not panic when under time pressure! Read each question very carefully to avoid careless mistakes

- When working through timed papers do not spend too long on one question. If the test is on paper you can always go back to a question. If it is an online test, check whether it will be possible to go back to questions

- Do not be afraid to write things down, but make sure your answer is clear

- You might not be able to complete all of the paper in the set time. Do not worry! Instead, use all of the time you have to work carefully and accurately.

60 mins

1 Give the next two numbers in these sequences:

a 6, 11, 17, 24, 32, ……………………………, ……………………………

b 144, 121, 100, 81, ……………………………, ……………………………

c 230, 250, 270, 290, ……………………………, ……………………………

3

2 Complete the grid so that each row and column adds up to 20.

2

6		10
		8
	5	

3 This graph shows the change in temperature of water in a kettle once it has started to heat up.

a How many seconds does it take for the water to reach boiling point?

……………………………

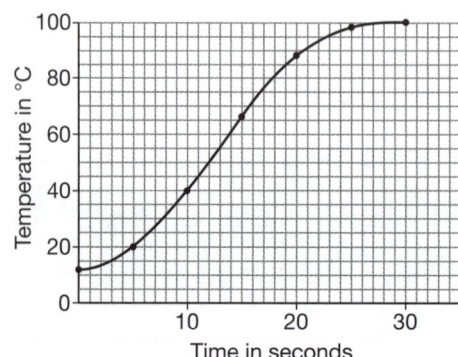

b Estimate the temperature of the water at the beginning. ·

c What was the temperature after 18 seconds? ·

3

In questions 4 to 7, which pattern on the right completes the grid on the left?

4

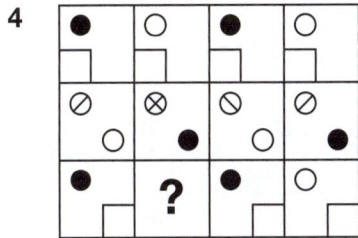

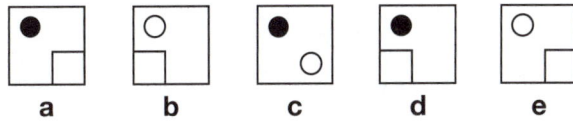

· 1

5

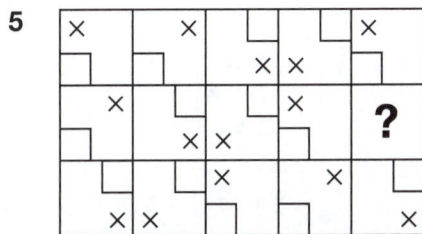

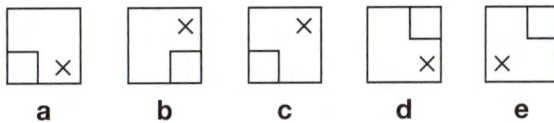

· 1

6

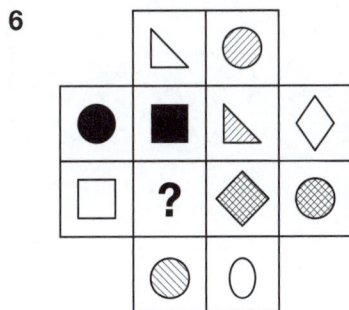

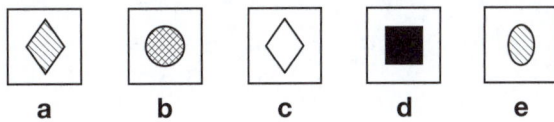

· 1

7

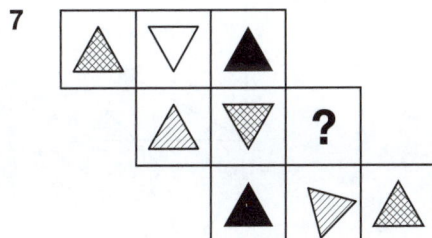

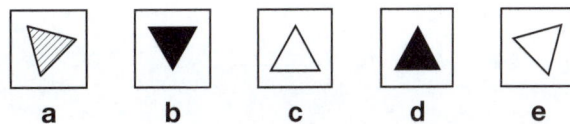

· 1

In questions 8 to 11, which shape or pattern on the left belongs to the group on the right?

8

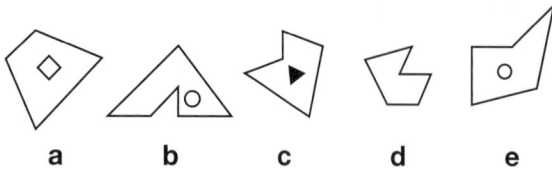

a   b   c   d   e

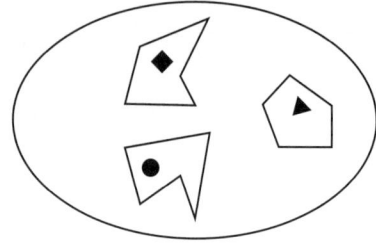

9

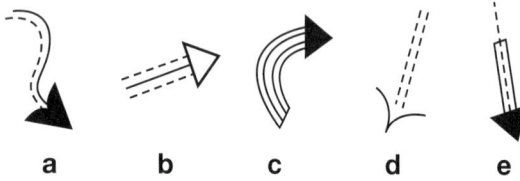

a   b   c   d   e

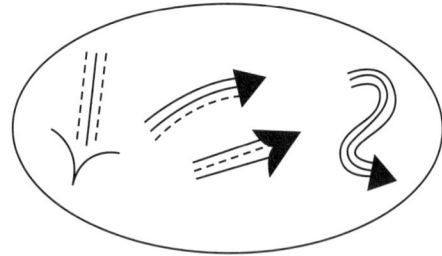

10

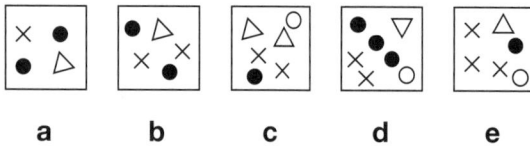

a   b   c   d   e

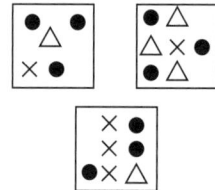

11

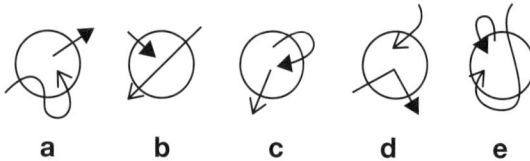

a   b   c   d   e

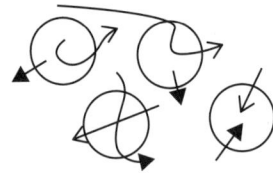

In questions 12 to 15, which pattern on the right is a reflection of the pattern on the left?

12

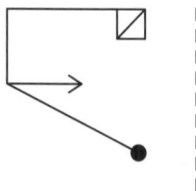

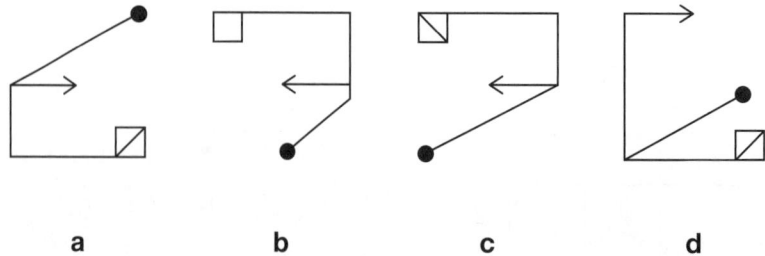

a   b   c   d

13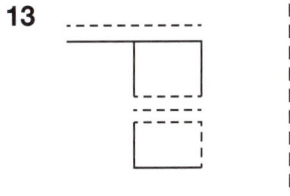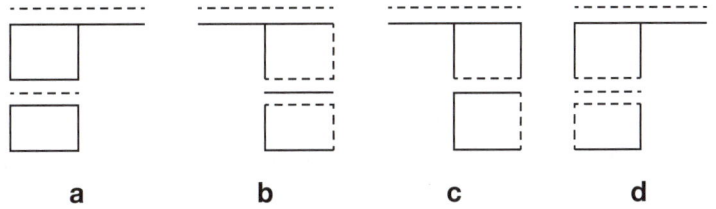

a   b   c   d

....

14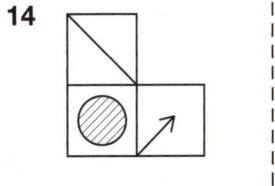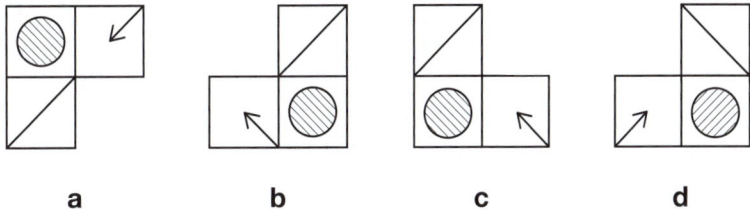

a   b   c   d

....

15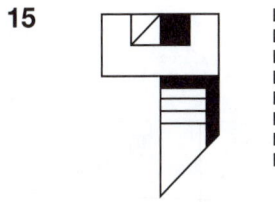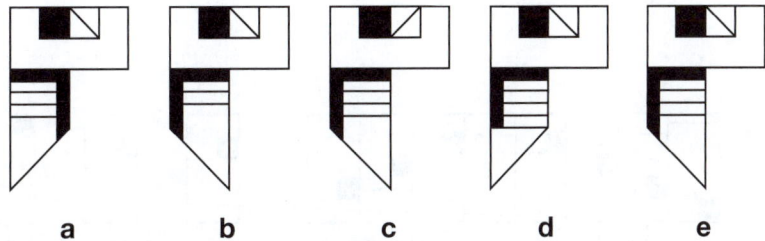

a   b   c   d   e

....

16 Write the number 401 067.5 in words.

....

17 Write the number thirteen hundred and three and thirteen hundredths in digits.

....

18 47 093 − 758 = ...

19 17 + 68 + 42 − 29 − 53 = ...

20 What is four hundred and twenty one less than six hundred and forty? ....

21 Give two numbers less than 50 that have 3, 4 and 6 as factors:

a.........................   b.........................

22 Which of the following numbers are multiples of four? Underline them.

14   32   52   68   82

In questions 23 to 26, which pattern on the right completes the sequence on the left?

23

a   b   c   d   e

....

24

a   b   c   d   e

....

25

a   b   c   d   e

....

26

a   b   c   d   e

....

27 What is a quarter of a half of 320? ....

28 Tilly buys a book for £2.50 and a snack for 45p.
She has now spent one-third of her pocket money.
How much pocket money did she have at the start? ....

29 $\frac{1}{4} \times 63.28 =$ ....

30 Complete the following:

$$\frac{4}{\Box} = \frac{16}{20} = \frac{\Box}{50}$$

31 Reduce the following fractions to their simplest form:

a $\dfrac{45}{60}$ = ... **b** $\dfrac{10}{14}$ = ... **c** $\dfrac{9}{21}$ = ... `1` ☐

32 What is the total of the digits in the tenths columns of the following three numbers:

    46.831   70.39   102.625   .... `1` ☐

33 7804.31 − 46.68 = ... `1` ☐

34 Complete the following table:

decimal	fraction	%
0.7		
		32%
	$\dfrac{3}{5}$	

`1` ☐

35 If $a = 5$ and $b = 7$, what is the value of $5a - 2b$? .... `1` ☐

36 $7x + 17 = 73$, $x =$ .... `1` ☐

37 $(6 \times 7) + (4^2 - 3) =$ .... `1` ☐

38 $102 - (56 \div 8) =$ .... `1` ☐

39 $5^3 + 7^2 - 3^3 =$ .... `1` ☐

40 What 3D shape has two flat circular faces and one curved face? .... `1` ☐

41 What type of quadrilateral has both pairs of opposite sides parallel but no right angles? .... `1` ☐

42 If two angles of a triangle are 43° and 78°, what is the size of the third angle? .... `1` ☐

43 What is the size of angle x and angle y in this diagram?

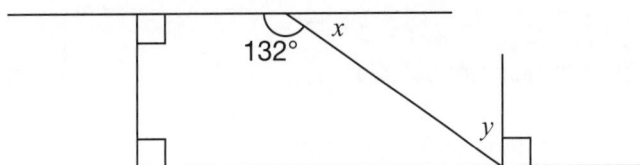

`1` ☐

44 What is the size of the base angles of an isosceles triangle if the third angle is 46°? **1**

45

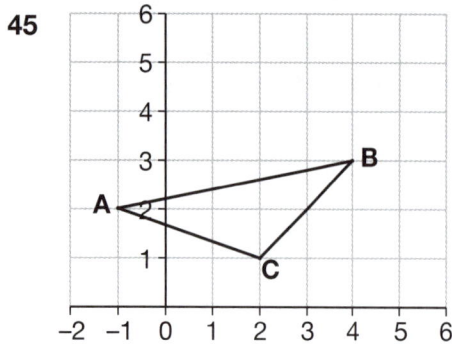

Translate the triangle **ABC** by 2 along the x axis and by 1 up the y axis, labelling the new positions A'B'C'. **1**

46 By how many degrees is the following pattern rotated in a clockwise direction?

....

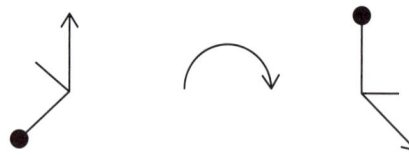

1

47 Reflect the shaded shape in the mirror line and draw its new position in the lower quadrant.

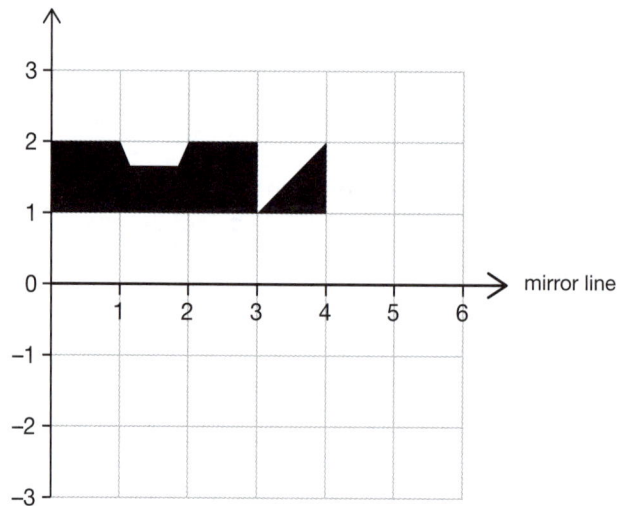

mirror line

1

48 What is the perimeter of a regular octagon if one side measures 4.5 cm? **1**

49

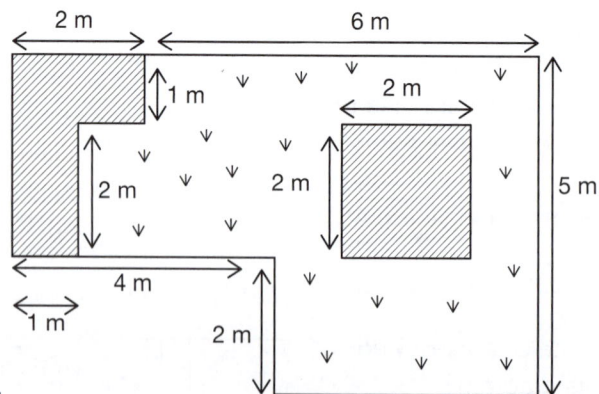

= flowerbed

v = grass lawn

From the diagram calculate:

a the total area of flower beds ....   **b** the area of the grass lawn **2**

50 A rectangular playing field is 85 m long and 25 m wide. If Kaz
runs round the very edge 4 times, how far does he run in total? . . . .

1

51 How many cm cubes can fit into a box that measures 50 cm × 12 cm × 5 cm? . . . .

1

52 A piece of wood is 4 m long and 0.5 m wide.
If its total volume is 1 cubic metre, what is its height? . . . .

1

53 The 7.15 p.m. bus started its journey 4 minutes late and has a further delay of
12 minutes on its way. It arrived at 8.23 p.m. What time should it have arrived?

. . . .

1

54 Convert these times to 24-hour format:

a 2.20 a.m. . . . . **b** 1.45 p.m. . . . .

c 9.05 p.m. . . . .

1

55 In a survey different families were asked about their favourite holiday destination.

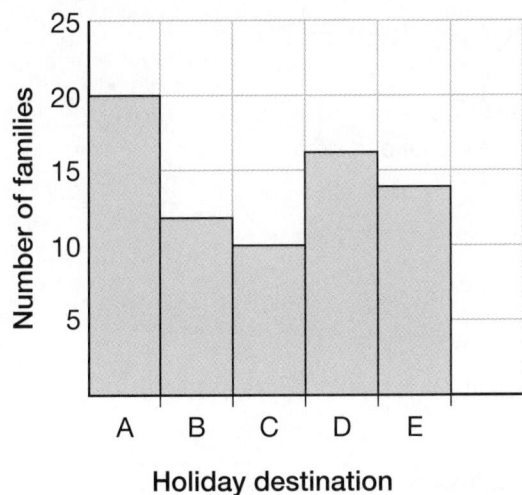

a How many families
were asked?   . . . .

1

b Which were the two most
popular destinations?

. . . .

1

56 Complete the bar graph below from the data shown in this tally chart:

Pineapple								
Lemon											
Cherry						
Plum									

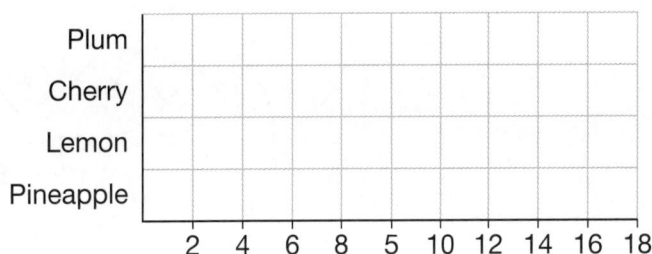

Test Paper 1

57

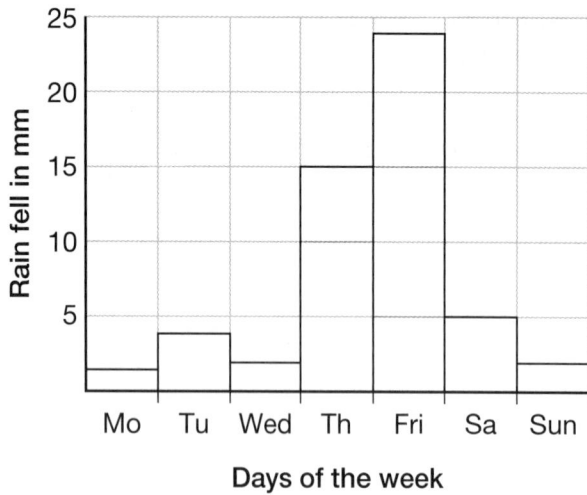

Days of the week

a How much rain fell altogether on the two wettest days? 1

b Which day was the driest? 1

58 A group of children chose one or more activity that they enjoy.
The results are shown in the diagram.

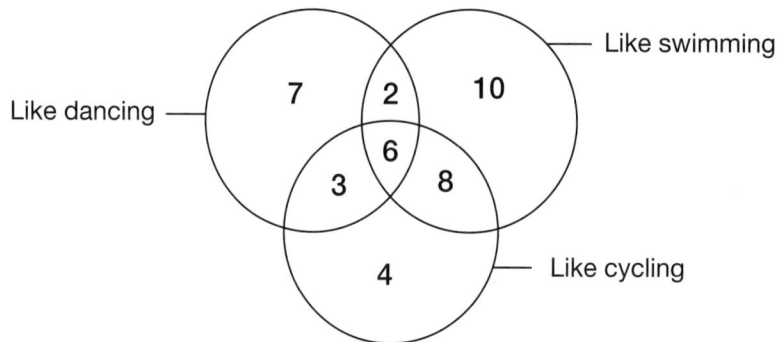

a How many children altogether have chosen swimming? 1

b How many children have only chosen one activity? 1

59 Packs of balls contain various combinations of different-coloured balls.

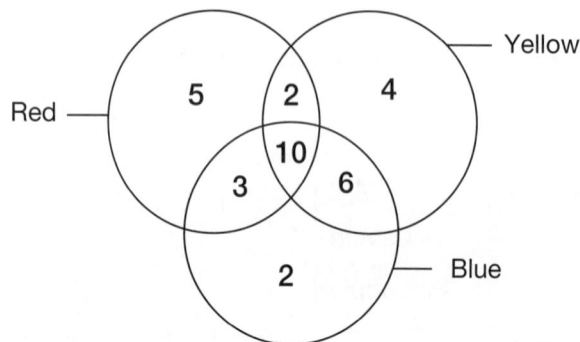

a How many packs contained red, yellow and blue? ....

b How many packs contained some blue balls? ....

60 In a class of 30 children 17 chose cheese sandwiches, and 24 chose orange juice. All except 5 of those who chose cheese sandwiches also chose orange juice. Show these results in the table:

	Chose cheese sandwich	Did not choose cheese sandwich
Chose orange juice		
Did not choose orange juice		

61 Children in a class were asked if they played the piano and if they were in a choir. These are the results:

	Play piano	Don't play piano
In a choir	8	12
Not in a choir	6	4

What fraction of the class of the class were in a choir? ....

62 What number comes next?

46   37   28   ?   ....

63 What number comes next?

3068   4079   5090   ?   ....

64 Give the next two terms in this pattern:

A5C9   B6D8   C7E7   ?   ....

65 Fill in the missing pattern:

840-Z   943-Y 1149-W   1252-V

Total
75

Test Paper 2

Test Papers

Test Paper 2

TOP TIP!

Before you start, think about the following:

- How did you get on with the previous paper?
- Is there anything you want to look up or check before starting this paper?
- Are there any words or facts that you need to double check before you start?

Then, when you feel ready, sit comfortably in a quiet place and start!

60 mins

For questions 1-4 underline the code which matches the shape or pattern given at the end of each line?

1

AX	BX	CY	CZ	?	AY	AZ	BY	BZ	CX
					a	b	c	d	e

2

DL	EM	DN	FM	?	DM	EL	EN	FL	FN
					a	b	c	d	e

3

BY	AX	CZ	BZ	?	AY	AZ	BX	CX	CY
					a	b	c	d	e

4

JC	LA	KC	KB	?	JA	JB	KA	LC	LB
					a	b	c	d	e

For questions 5-9 underline the shape or pattern which completes the second pair in the same way as the first pair.

5

(is to ⊚ as ⟨ is to

a   b   c   d   e

6 |= is to |≡| as ‖| is to

                 a   **b**   **c**   **d**   **e**

7 ●–◐–◐–● is to ●–● as (vertical line of dots) is to

                 a   **b**   **c**   **d**   **e**

8 Z is to ⊐ as N is to

                 a   **b**   **c**   **d**   **e**

9 (right triangle) is to (3 dots vertical) as (pentagon) is to

                 a   **b**   **c**   **d**   **e**

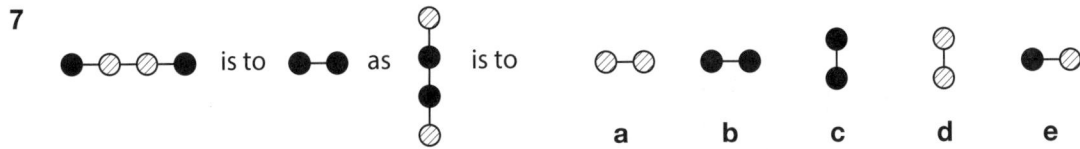

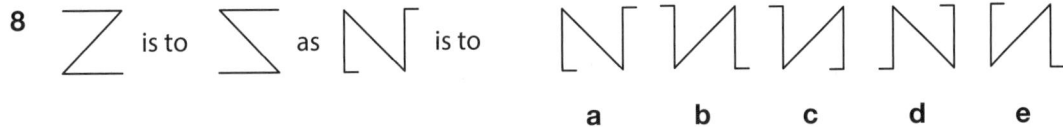

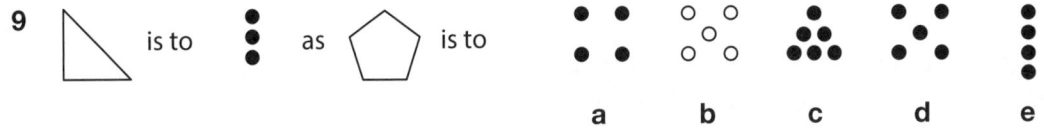

In questions 10 to 13 underline the shape or pattern on the right that belongs to the group on the left.

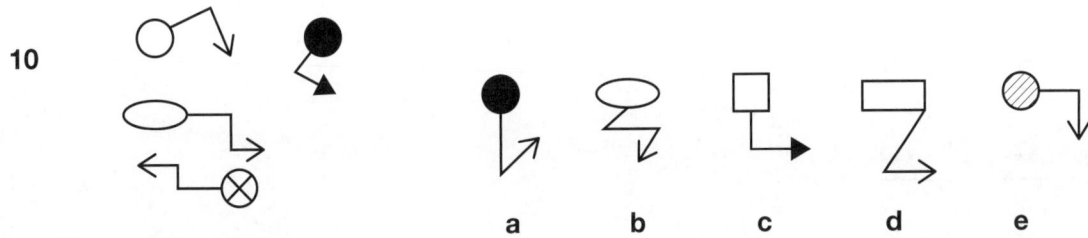

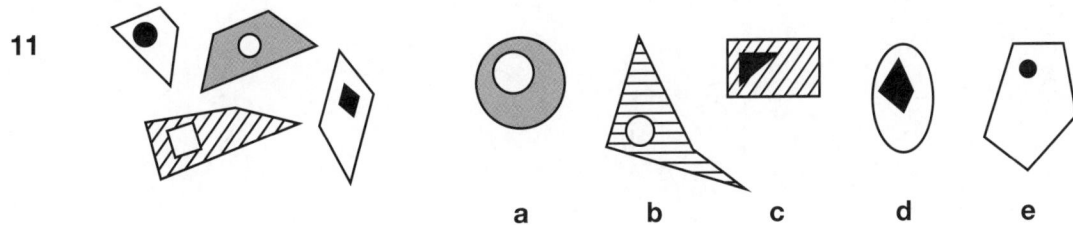

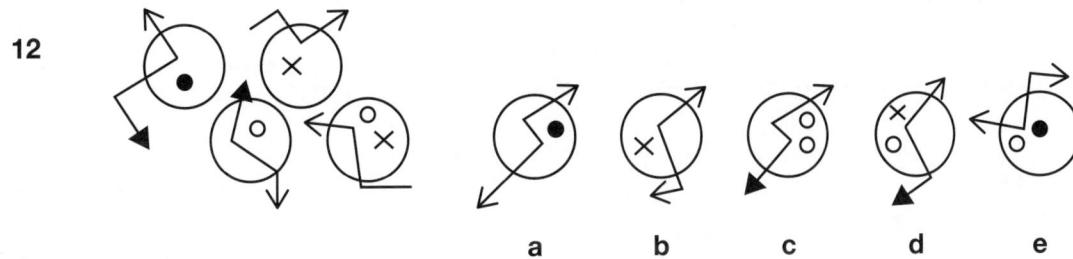

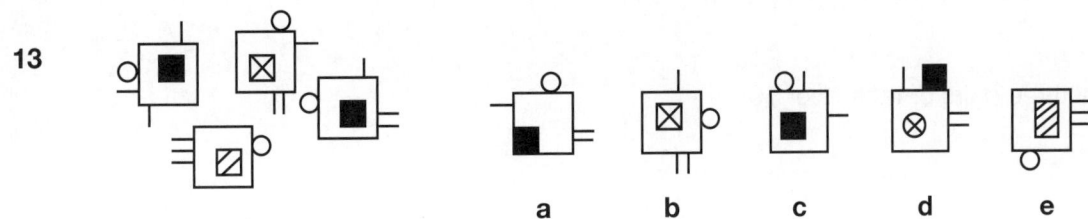

10

                 a   **b**   **c**   **d**   **e**

11

                 a   **b**   **c**   **d**   **e**

12

                 a   **b**   **c**   **d**   **e**

13

                 a   **b**   **c**   **d**   **e**

4

4

14 The bar graph shows the amount of time Tim spent reading each day for a week.

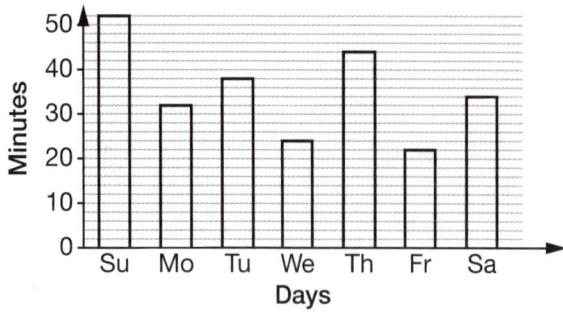

a On which days did Tim read for less than half an hour?.......................... ☐ 1

b For how many more minutes did he read on Sunday than on Friday? .... ☐ 1

c What was the total amount of time Tim spent
reading at the weekend (Sunday and Saturday)? .... ☐ 1

15 Work out the missing numbers in this addition sum:

3	**a**	7
b	2	5
5	1	2

a .... **b** .... ☐ 1

16 Write the number 4 602 015 in words... ☐ 1

17 Write the number six million and sixty-six in digits................................ ☐ 1

18 5807 + 694 = ... ☐ 1

19 What number is 592 less than one thousand?...................................... ☐ 1

20 Give three pairs of factors of 56.

.... ☐ 1

21 Which of these numbers are multiples of 9? Underline them.

89   72   64   180   190   279

In questions 22 to 25 which net on the right can be folded to give the cube on the left?

22

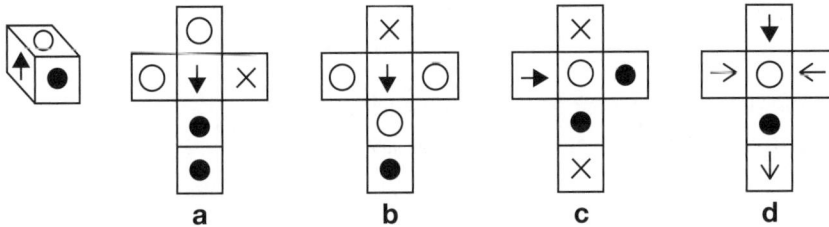

a   b   c   d

23

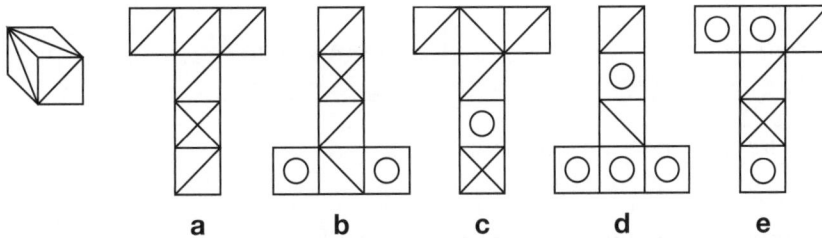

a   b   c   d   e

24

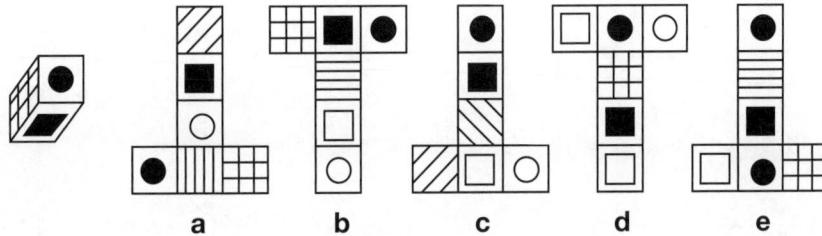

a   b   c   d   e

25

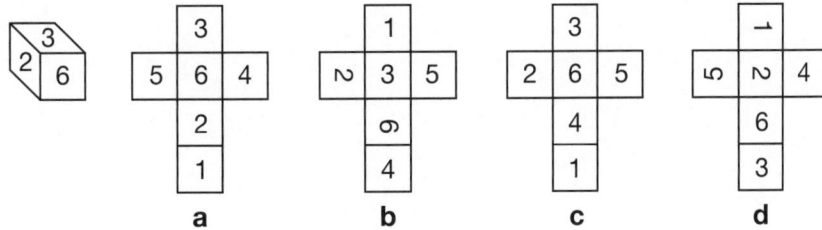

a   b   c   d

26 Write down the prime numbers between 20 and 30. ....

27 $5^2 + 7^2 + 2^3 =$ ....

28 What is the difference between 5^2 and 5^3? ....

29 Give two prime numbers that add together to give 30. ....

30 $5006.45 - 3703.77 =$ ....

31 What is the total of three point six four two and fifty-five and five hundredths?

.... 1

32 What is 65% of £360? 1

33 If 15% of a sum is £105, what is the full sum? 1

34 If the average weekly cost of groceries for a family is £120,
what is the new average cost if prices increase by 5%? 1

35 In a sale, prices are reduced by 20%. What is the sale price of:

 a a dress at £75? .... **b** a jacket at £30? 2

36 Give 0.168 as a fraction in its lowest terms. 1

37 Convert these improper fractions to mixed numbers:

 a $\dfrac{26}{4}$ .... **b** $\dfrac{17}{3}$ .... **c** $\dfrac{19}{7}$ 1

38 What is $6a - 4b$ if $a = 8$ and $b = 5$? 1

39 $9x + 53 = 134$, $x =$ 1

40 $(45 - 6) + (4 \times 7) =$ 1

41 $4^2 + (3 \times 4) - 3^2 =$ 1

42 $3 \times 4 \times 5 + (2^3 - 3) =$ 1

43 What 3D shape has 8 edges and 5 faces? 1

44

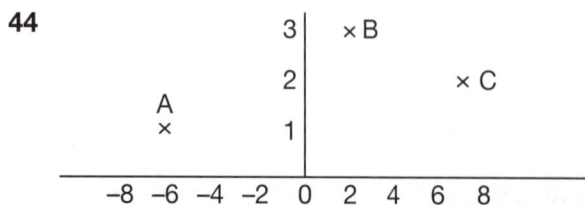

Give the coordinates of the points A, B and C. 1

45 Plot, label and join the following points on the graph below
and give the name of the quadrilateral that is formed. ....

2

W (2,2)   X (4,7)   Y (5,7)   Z (7,2)

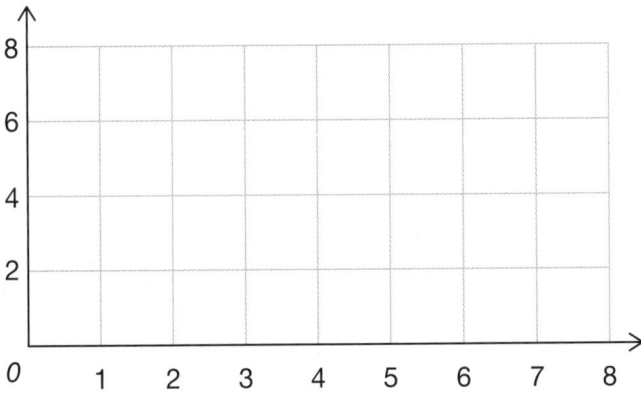

46 Plot and label a point C so that when joined to point A and to point B it forms an
isosceles triangle with line AB at the base. Give the coordinates of point C.

1

....

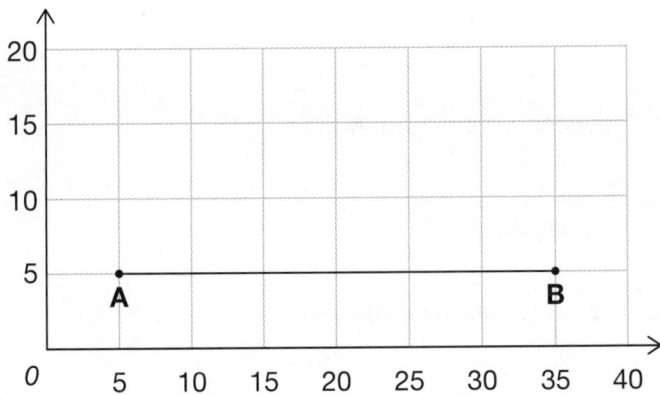

47 How many mm in 1 m and 73 cm? ....

1

48 Order the following measurements from smallest to largest:

1.5 km   1750 m   0.707 km   770 m   ....

1

49 How many seconds in 1 hour 4 minutes and 20 sec? ....

1

50 What is the area of a rectangle 6 cm wide if it is twice as long as it is wide?

....

1

51 A pentagon has one side of 12 cm, the other
sides are all 9 cm long. What is its perimeter? .... `1`

52 If 100 g of grass seed is needed to cover a one metre square area
of lawn, how much seed is needed for the lawn shown in this plan? .... `1`

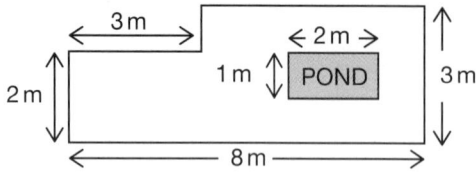

53 What is the volume of a storage unit 4 m long, 3 m wide and 1.5 m high? .... `1`

54 The top surface of a tall box is 500 cm².
If its total volume is 1 m³, what is its height? .... `1`

Use this timetable to answer questions 55 and 56:

Station	Train A	Train B	Train C	Train D
Tappin	05:35	09:50	13:30	17:15
Warton	06:10	10:20	14:05	17:50
Flinting	06:48	10:42	14:37	18:20

55 Which train has the quickest journey between Tappin and Warton? .... `1`

56 If train C is delayed by 25 minutes between
Warton and Flinting, when will it arrive at Flinting? .... `1`

57 The graph shows the distance covered by a runner over four hours

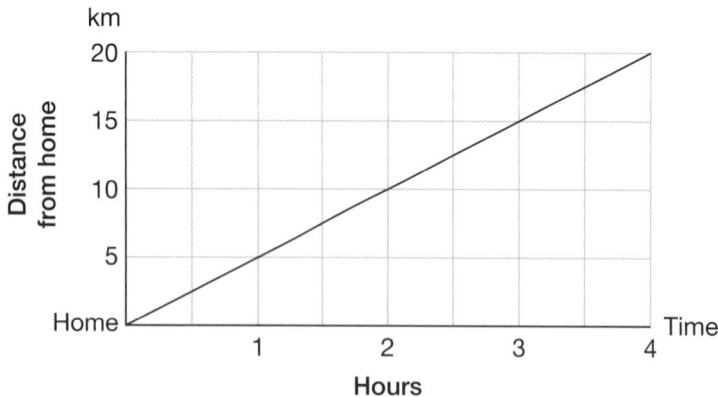

a How far from home was the runner after 1½ hours? .... `1`

b After how many minutes did the runner take a rest? .... `1`

58

temp °c

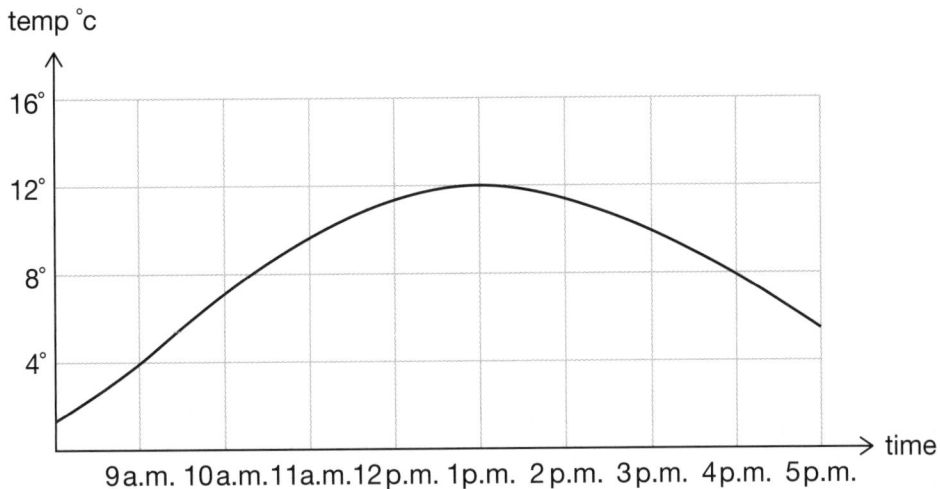

By how much did the temperature drop between 1 p.m. and 4 p.m.?

....

1

59

◯ represents 2 cars

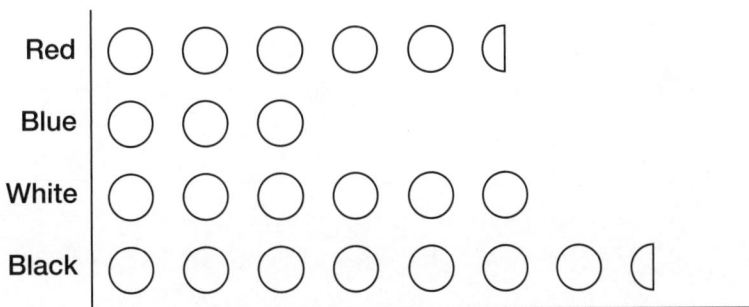

Red	◯ ◯ ◯ ◯ ◯ ◖
Blue	◯ ◯ ◯
White	◯ ◯ ◯ ◯ ◯ ◯
Black	◯ ◯ ◯ ◯ ◯ ◯ ◯ ◖

This is a record of the different colours of cars in a
car park. How many cars were recorded altogether? ....

1

60

⌀ represents 4 plants

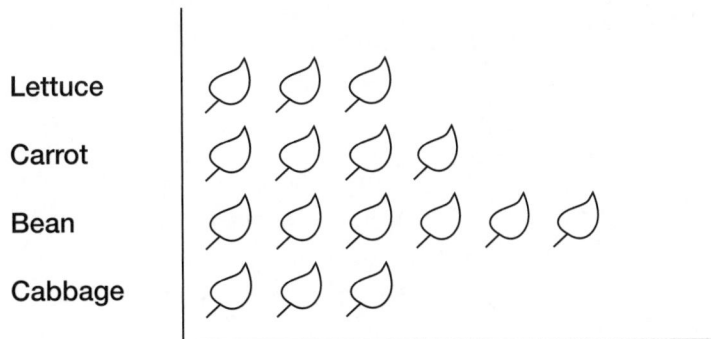

Lettuce	⌀ ⌀ ⌀
Carrot	⌀ ⌀ ⌀ ⌀
Bean	⌀ ⌀ ⌀ ⌀ ⌀ ⌀
Cabbage	⌀ ⌀ ⌀

These vegetable plants were bought by
Mr Smith for his allotment. How many more
bean plants than lettuces did Mr Smith buy? ....

1

In questions 61 to 64, which pattern on the right completes the grid on the left? Underline your answer.

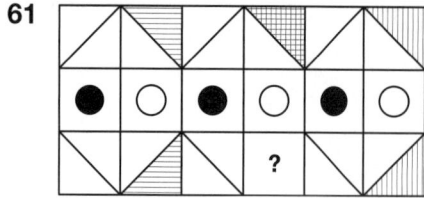

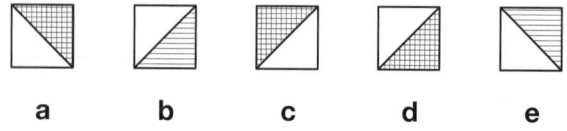

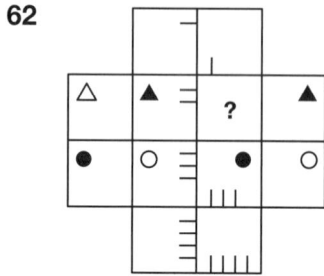

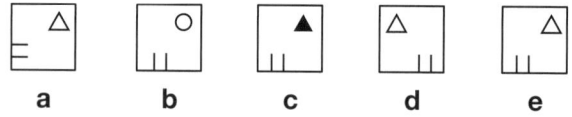

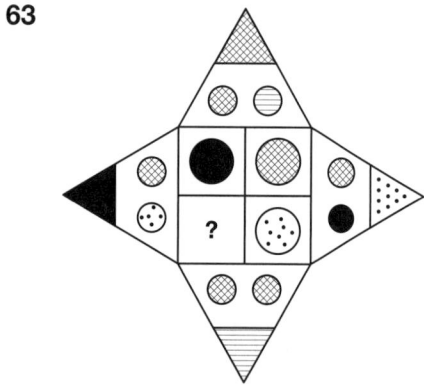

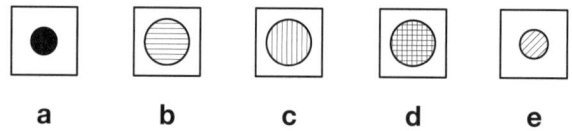

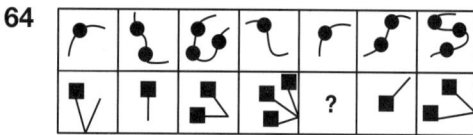

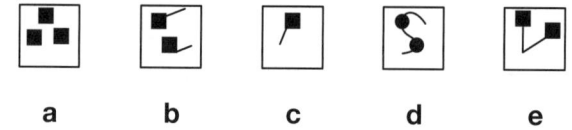

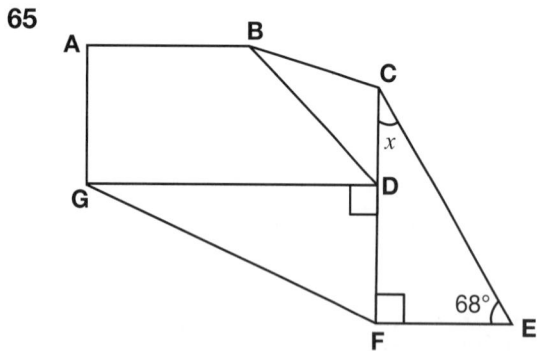

61

a   b   c   d   e

62

a   b   c   d   e

63

a   b   c   d   e

64

a   b   c   d   e

4

65

a What type of shape is **ABDG**?

....

b What is the value of angle x?

....

2

Total
70

Keywords

Some special words and symbols are used in this book. You will find them in **bold** when they appear in the Papers. These words are explained here.

|---|---|
area	The surface or amount of two-dimensional space taken up by a shape or object
clockwise	A rotational movement in the same direction as the movement of the hands of a clock
cubed number	A number multiplied by itself twice
cubic centimetre	A unit used to measure volume
cubic metre	A unit used to measure volume
equivalent fraction	Fractions written in different denominators, but with the same value, for example $\frac{1}{2}$ and $\frac{2}{4}$
factor	A factor is a number that can divide exactly into another number with no remainder, e.g. 3 is a factor of 9
graph	A pictorial representation or a diagram that presents data or values in an organised way
hexagon	A 2D flat shape with 6 straight sides
multiple	A number that can be divided by another number without a remainder
percentage	Indicates hundredths, for example 5% is $\frac{5}{100}$
perimeter	The distance around the edge of a shape
points of a compass	The directions shown on a compass. These include north, south, east, west and the points in-between: north-east, south-east, north-west and south-west
prime number	A number that can only be divided exactly by 1 and the number itself.
product	A number or a quantity that you get by multiplying two or more numbers or expressions together
rectangle	A quadrilateral that has four right angles and opposite sides equal in length
rotate	In mathematics this means to turn an object clockwise or anticlockwise around a given fixed point
round	roughly or approximately, for example 42 rounded to the nearest 10 is 40, 470 rounded to the nearest 100 is 500
squared number	A number multiplied by itself
symmetry	When two or more parts are identical after a flip or turn. The simplest type of symmetry is a reflection, or mirror image
tally chart	A simple way of recording and counting frequencies, with each occurrence shown by a tally mark where every fifth tally is a horizontal line through the previous four vertical lines, making a set of five
translate	A translation in mathematics moves a shape left or right and/or up or down. The translated shapes look exactly the same size as the original shape
volume	The space taken up by a solid object, which is that same as its capacity

Keywords

Essentials

- Don't worry too much about the level that you start at. Beginning with an easier book can help your confidence.
- Make sure you have the right equipment – you will need your pencils, an eraser, and a notebook.
- This book contains skills guidance and worked examples, but if you need more help with technique, the Bond Handbooks might also be useful to you.

Studying Effectively

1 Turn to the first topic and read the Key Skills box. You might want to read it a few times or with someone else to understand it properly or to underline key words.

2 Read the worked example a few times and make sure you understand it.

3 In your notebook, write down the topic heading and the worked example on a new page. This is for you to revise and remember. Once you have completed the final book, you will have a super-useful notebook that you can use in secondary school.

4 Now set a timer – a kitchen timer, a watch or phone with an alarm – for the timed section.

5 Work your way through the questions carefully. If you don't know the answer to something, draw a circle around the question number and take your best guess. This is important as you can find patterns if you make mistakes and it highlights where you need to consolidate.

6 Ask someone to mark the paper for you or mark it yourself and see where you made mistakes. Is there a common pattern? For every mistake, decide if it is not knowing the technique properly, not consolidating the technique enough or a loss of focus and label this next to each question using T = technique, C = consolidation, F = focus.

7 Have another go at the questions you made errors in to understand what you did wrong. If it is vocabulary problem, write down the word with its meaning / synonym / antonym at the back of your book so that you widen your vocabulary range.

Making Mistakes

Everyone makes mistakes and they are an important part of how we learn. The reason we practise before an exam is so that we can make those mistakes in a safe space rather than in the test itself and that way we can learn from them and make fewer mistakes when it really matters.

Remember that there is no such thing as a 'silly mistake'. You are not silly, and neither is your mistake. It is usually not understanding the technique, not consolidating the skill needed so that it is only partially remembered, or you have lost focus. Losing focus does not mean that you have done something bad, it just means that your attention was on something else. These tips can help:

Not Understanding the Technique:

• Go back to the learning section and reread the key skills box.

• Look at the worked example that you have in your notebook.

• Use the Bond Handbook for more support.

Not Consolidating Enough:

• It is amazing how much consolidation is needed by everyone so don't worry about doing lots of additional questions.

• Look at Bond online for some more questions to help you revise.

• Ask someone to test you on the technique.

Losing Focus:

• Make sure that you are not too tired, hungry, thirsty or distracted.

• Work out where you have made a mistake and break it down into sections. It might be that you focus on tricky division, but go too fast when it comes to addition. It might be that you read the comprehension extract, but you lost focus and misread it.

• Once you have identified the problem area, make sure that in new questions, you check yourself and focus carefully.

Common Problems

'I don't have time to study.'

Make sure that you have a timetable that is doable. If you have lots of activities that take up time, perhaps break your work up. The books all have timing sections so fit in smaller sections when you can. It's important to talk to your parent if you feel that you need more time for your 11+ work.

'I find it hard to complete my homework as I want to play instead.'

Motivation is difficult for most people. Don't completely stop all fun activities during the 11+ but get a balance. Key to this is a timetable so you know when, what and where to study. Make sure it is doable and build in something fun if you complete your homework for the day. Another tip is to write down your reasons for doing the 11+. It might be to keep your family happy, to get into a school your friends are going to, or even that the school is convenient. Ask yourself how important each reason is. Can you commit to the reasons you have? If so, keep remembering the reason and what will happen if you don't commit? Perhaps talk to your family so that they know how you feel.

'My friend is using different books to me.'

The Bond 11+ system covers English/Verbal Reasoning and Maths/Non-verbal reasoning/spatial awareness. Bond has had many decades of success in 11+ material. Many tutors will only use Bond for their pupils, and they get an exceptionally high pass rate. It doesn't mean that Bond is the only 11+ provider, so don't worry that your friend is using different material. What is important is that you are fully prepared for your CEM online exam, and you can have confidence in the Bond system.

'I'm scared of failing.'

It is natural to feel that. Remember that you cannot climb a mountain in one gigantic step. You need lots and lots of little steps to get to the top. The 11⁺ is like that. You can't sit down and learn everything straight away, but the little steps you take will lead you to the exam. Remember that every mistake can be identified and once you identify it, you may be able to understand it and solve the problem for next time. Mistakes are perfection in progress! If a selective school is the best learning environment for you, then you can work little and often through the books and then test papers leading up to the exam. If you find it too much and you are working at your full potential already, then maybe a school that is not selective will suit your learning better. There is no 'best school' and 'worst school' for everyone. It is the best school for an individual child. Do talk to someone about your feelings though as you need to feel supported.

'My friend has a tutor. Do I need one?'

Whether or not to have tutor depends on many different factors, including where your particular strengths and challenges lie, your own approach to learning, and whether your parents are comfortable with the costs involved. The Bond system is rigorous and aims to support every child with a range of books and learning materials. The Bond Handbooks can do the job of a tutor and many tutors also use the Bond books and Handbooks with their pupils. Bond has been providing 11⁺ material since the 1960s, helping thousands of pupils to pass their 11⁺ exams without having a tutor.

'I don't want to do the 11⁺ exam.'

This is a conversation to have with your family, but the best advice might be to follow the 11⁺ books anyway. They will teach you skills, techniques and methods that will give you self-confidence regardless of the secondary school you attend. No knowledge is a waste, and you will be keeping your options open.

There is more information on the Bond website. Bond has a Parent's Guide to the 11⁺ and there is a range of supportive printed and online material. See online for further details: **www.bond11plus.co.uk**

Answers

Learning Paper 1: Special Numbers & Place Value

1 **−9°C** 6 − 15 = −9. A jump of 6 takes you to zero and then another 9 to −9.

2 **Eight million, one hundred and four thousand, five hundred and nineteen**

3 **4 032 302**

4–5 When rounding to the nearest hundred look at the number in the tens column. If it is 5 or more, increase the hundreds by one. If it is less than 5, the hundreds are unchanged. Zeros are added to the tens and ones columns. When rounding to the nearest ten the same rules apply, but look at the tens column, and look at the tenths column when rounding to the nearest whole number. Zeros do not need to be added when rounding to the nearest whole number.

4 a **98 100; 98 100**   b **191 900; 191 890**

5 a **49 600**   b **50 000**   c **49 599**

6 **975 936 < 978 794 < 980 203 < 980 212** When ordering numbers begin by looking at the digits in the first column on the left, then the next column and so on. Here, all of the numbers start with 9, so look at the next column – 7s come before 8s, then 75 comes before 78. If the digits are the same in the next column move on until there is a difference. For example **980 2**03 **980 2**12 – here the first 4 digits are the same, so it is the number in the tens column that shows which number is smaller: 980 2**0**3 <980 2**1**2.

7 **−3** 25 + 32 = 57; the difference between 57 and 60 is 3; 60 is greater than 57, and as the answer is below zero it is a negative number −3.

8 **−26°C** If the temperature goes up it will be less cold, 6 degrees warmer than −21°C is −15°C. The temperature then goes down 11 degrees so it will be colder; 11 degrees colder than −15°C is −26°C.

9 **27 643** Total means adding together, 24 560 + 2078 = 26 638, then 26 638 + 1005 = 27 643

10 **2**   Factors of a number divide into the number exactly with no remainder. Of the numbers given, only 2 goes into 34 exactly (34 ÷ 2 = 17).

11 **3 and 16, 4 and 12, 6 and 8** All these numbers will divide into 48: 3 x 16 = 48; 4 x 12 = 48; 6 x 8 = 48.

12 *Any 3 of:* **45, 60, 75, 90** A multiple of 15 is the product of 15 times any other whole number, e.g. 15 × 2 = 30, 15 × 3 = **45**, 15 × 4 = **60**, 15 × 5 = **75**, 15 × 6 = **90**, 15 × 7 = 105 etc. Four of these multiples are between 31 and 100.

13 48 **64** 72 **98** **106** If a number can be divided exactly by 6 it is a multiple of 6. If there is a remainder it is not a multiple. So 48 ÷ 6 = 8 yes, 64 ÷ 6 = 10 R4 no, 72 ÷ 6 = 12 yes, 98 ÷ 6 = 16 R2 no, 106 ÷ 6 = 17 R4 no, the question asks for those that are not a multiple

14 **800** 32 rows of 25 is 32 × 25 = 800 (32 × 20 = 640) + (32 × 5 = 160); 640 + 160 = 800

15 **46 teams with 3 left out** Divide 325 by 7 to find out how many complete teams there will be: 325 ÷ 7 = 46 R3. The remainder is the number of pupils left out.

16 **3** (36 ÷ 3 = 12, 54 ÷ 3 = 18, 78 ÷ 3 = 26, 105 ÷ 3 = 35)

17 **5** Begin by working out 147 ÷ 7 = 21 and 4^2 = 16; then write as a missing number sentence; 16 + ? = 21;16 + 5 = 21

18 **89** Any number squared is multiplied by itself, so $5^2 + 8^2$ = (5 × 5) + (8 × 8) = 25 + 64 = 89

19 **13** A prime number can only be divided exactly by itself and one; even numbers greater than 2 can always be divided by 2 so they cannot be prime. So 4, 10 and 18 are not prime numbers; 15 and 21 can be divided by 3 so they are not prime; 13 can only be divided by 1 and 13.

20 Underlined numbers: **2, 13, 31, 17**
Circled numbers: **9, 27**

21 **369** The others are cube numbers: 1 = 1 × 1 × 1, 27 = 3 × 3 × 3, 125 = 5 × 5 × 5, 512 = 8 × 8 × 8, 1000 = 10 × 10 × 10

22 **64**

Learning Paper 2: Logic, Sequences and Grids

1 Look at the difference between each term and apply it to the last term to find the next number:

a **76** The numbers decrease by 11 each time; 87 − 11 = 76

b **43** The numbers increase by 7 each time; 36 + 7 = 43

c **9060** The numbers decrease by 1010 each time; 10 070 − 1010 = 9060

d **49** The numbers decrease by 5 each time; 54 − 5 = 49

e **31** The difference between the numbers increases by 1 each time (10 + 1 = 11; 11+ 2 = 13; 13 + 3 = 16; 16 + 4 = 20; 20 + 5 = 25 and 25 + 6 = 31)

2 **d** The number of lines increases along each row, so the missing pattern will have 3 vertical lines.

3 **c** The shading of the circles follows a sequence of black-white-black-cross from left to right with the pattern continuing in successive rows of the grid. So the missing square will have a circle with a cross; the short lines are in the same position along each row.

4 **b** The patterns in the central squares are the same as the patterns in the outer triangles of that same quarter of the grid, so the missing square will have a white circle.

5 **a** The pattern in the first square of the top and the bottom row are repeated along the row, so the missing square will have a smaller square with top left and bottom right corners in black.

6 **c** The whole grid is made up of a symmetrical pattern with each quarter a reflection of the adjacent quarter. So the missing square will have a small square in the top left and bottom right corners with diagonal lines from top left to bottom right. It will also have a white circle in both the top right and bottom left corner and a black circle in the centre.

7 **d** Each square is divided in half with alternate halves shaded along the row; shading lines alternate between horizontal and vertical; the square is halved in the same way along each row. So the missing square has a diagonal line from top left to bottom right and the triangle on the right shaded with vertical lines.

8 **a** The outer squares have a circle with the inner half shaded in the same way as the opposite triangle of the central square. So the missing square has a circle halved with a horizontal line and the top half is shaded with vertical lines.

9 **e** The cross moves clockwise around the corners of the outer squares and the shapes in the corners of the central square are repeated in the adjacent corners of the outer squares. So the missing square will have a cross in the top right corner and a white circle in the bottom left corner.

10 **d** In each row and each column there are squares with either 1, 2 or 3 dots, the diagonal direction of the line alternates along the row, and the shading of the circles is the same along each row. So the missing square will have 1 white circle in the middle.

11 **c** The triangles rotate 90 degrees anticlockwise and the central pattern repeats – cross, black circle, white circle – along the sequence. So the next image will have the right angle of the triangle in the bottom left corner and a white circle inside.

12 **d** The number of horizontal lines alternates between 1 and 2 and the shading of the circle repeats – cross, white circle, black circle. So the next image will have 2 horizontal lines above a black circle.

13 **e** The square U-shape rotates 90 degrees anticlockwise and the number of black spots decreases by 1 along the sequence. So the next image will be an upside down U-shape with 6 black spots.

14 **a** The arrow line rotates 45 degrees anticlockwise along the sequence, so it will point to the top right in the next image.

15 **c** The line shading in 1 direction is followed by shading lines at right angles to those lines in the next square, with both lines in the third square forming a grid. So the next square will have diagonal line shading from top left to bottom right.

16 **b** The lower 2 lines remain the same, the top line rotates approximately 30 degrees anticlockwise. So the next image will have the top line pointing up 30 degrees above the left-pointing horizontal line.

17 **d** The circles alternate between being divided into 4 or 6 sections; the shading of the sixths rotates anticlockwise. So the next image with be a circle divided into 6, with the lower left sixth shaded black.

18 **d** The sequence is made up of sets of 3 of the same shape. The first has a plain line, the second has an outer dotted line added, and the third image has a third plain outer line added. So the next shape will be a circle with a plain line and a second dotted outer line.

19 **a** The pattern of shapes repeats along the sequence – circle, comma, heart, 2 circles – and the shading follows a repeating pattern of diagonal lines – white, black. So the next image will be 2 white circles.

20 **9 days** Number of 5 ml doses = 135 ÷ 5 = 27; number of days = number of doses ÷ 3 = 27 ÷ 3 = 9

21 **a** **45, 52** 15 × 3 = 45, 45 + 7 = 52
   b **515, 508** 103 × 5 = 515, 515 − 7 = 508

22 **a** **200 g** the amount of butter to sugar is 150 : 120 = 15 : 12 = 5 : 4 So the sugar needed for 250 g butter is $\frac{4}{5}$ × 250 = 200 g

   b **40** If 120 g sugar makes 24 biscuits, 120 ÷ 24 g = 5 g sugar per biscuit, so 200 g ÷ 5 = 40

23 *(1 mark for 3 correct answers)*
   Find the easiest gap to complete first – it might not be the first one.
   Start with b – what minus 4 gives 2? Answer: 6. If **b is 6** then **a is a multiply sign (×)** as 3 × 6 = 18. Then look at the middle row – what minus 4 is 4? Answer: 8. If **d is 8** then **e is 3 × 8 = 24** and on the bottom row 24 − 2 = 22, so **f is 22.** Then how can 18 and 4 make 22? By adding them together, so **c is a +** sign.
   a ×
   b 6
   c +
   d 8
   e 24
   f 22

3	×	6	=	18
×		−		+
8	−	4	=	4
=		=		=
24	−	2	=	22

24 **50** Number of boats starting = 18 + 32 + 11 = 61; 61 minus the 5 that capsize = 56; 56 minus the 6 abandoning the race = 50

25 **8 weeks.** Number of sacks per week is 210 ÷ 7 = 30; number of weeks from 240 sacks is 240 ÷ 30 = 8

Learning Paper 3: Number Skills

1 **245** 735 ÷ 3 = 245

2 **20** $\frac{1}{2}$ of 100 = 50 red beads and $\frac{1}{4}$ of 100 = 25 blue beads; 100 − 50 − 25 = 25 beads left; $\frac{1}{5}$ of 25 = 5 white beads and 25 − 5 = 20 beads left that are green.

3 **280** One-quarter is 210 ÷ 3 = 70, so a whole is 70 × 4 = 280

4 $\frac{2}{7}$ The other fractions simplify to give $\frac{1}{7}$; $\frac{4}{28} = \frac{1}{7}$; $\frac{7}{49} = \frac{1}{7}$; $\frac{5}{35} = \frac{1}{7}$

5 $\frac{2}{8}, \frac{3}{12}, \frac{5}{20}$

6 $\frac{11}{99}, \frac{2}{9}, \frac{6}{18}, \frac{21}{27}$ To compare values change so fractions all have the same denominator: $\frac{11}{99} = \frac{1}{9}$; $\frac{6}{18} = \frac{3}{9}$; $\frac{21}{27} = \frac{7}{9}$

7 $\frac{9}{10}$ (accept $\frac{18}{20}$) Change all the fractions so they have the same denominator then add the numerators: $\frac{2}{5} = \frac{8}{20}$ and $\frac{3}{10} = \frac{6}{20}$; $\frac{8}{20} + \frac{4}{20} + \frac{6}{20}$ $= \frac{18}{20}$ which simplifies to $\frac{9}{10}$

8 $\frac{5}{12}$ Express as twelfths then subtract the numerators: $\frac{1}{6} = \frac{2}{12}$ and $\frac{1}{3} = \frac{4}{12}$; $\frac{11}{12} - \frac{2}{12} - \frac{4}{12} = \frac{5}{12}$

9 $7\frac{5}{7}$ As these are all in sevenths, add the numerators $3 + 6 + 45 = 54$; divide by 7: $54 \div 7 = 7$ R5 which is $7\frac{5}{7}$

10 $2\frac{1}{6}$ Express all as twelfths: $\frac{3}{4} = \frac{9}{12}$; $\frac{3}{6} = \frac{6}{12}$; $\frac{11}{12}$; add the numerators $9 + 6 + 11 = 26$; divide by 12: $26 \div 12 = 2$ R2 which is $2\frac{2}{12}$; $\frac{2}{12}$ can be simplified to $\frac{1}{6}$ so $2\frac{2}{12}$ and $2\frac{1}{6}$ are both acceptable answers

11 3 Creams are $\frac{1}{4} \times 28 = 7$; gingers are $\frac{1}{7} \times 28 = 4$; chocolate are $\frac{1}{2} \times 28 = 14$; wafers are $28 - 7 - 4 - 14 = 3$

12 10 If black cars are $\frac{1}{3}$ of the total, then the blue and red cars must be $\frac{2}{3}$; $16 + 4 = 20$ so $\frac{2}{3} = 20$; divide 20 by 2 to find $\frac{1}{3}$: $20 \div 2 = 10$

13 a £4.08 $1.25 + 1.05 + (0.89 \times 2) = 2.30 + 1.78 = 4.08$
   b 50p, 20p, 20p, 2p $5.00 - 4.08 = 0.92$. Start by subtracting the largest coin possible in this number 92p – 50p = 42p, then the next coin down: 42p – 20p = 22p; this can be repeated 22p – 20p = 2p

14 3001.161

3	0	⁰4̶	¹0	.	¹2	¹0	1
			9	.	0	4	
3	0	0	1	.	1	6	1

15 £6.75 If 1 euro = 90p, then 7 euros = £6.30 (as 7 x 90p = 630p); 0.50 euros is the same as $\frac{1}{2}$ euro so divide 90p by 2 (90p ÷ 2 = 45p); then add £6.30 and 45p to find 7.50 euros (£6.30 + £0.45 = £6.75)

16 £4.95 The cost of 6 individual DVDs is £4.99 × 6 = £29.94; the difference in price is £29.94 – £24.99 = £4.95

17 442.59 simple addition – keep the decimal points in line.

18 5.00 Refer to page 12 on sequences; subtract to find the difference of 0.15 each time; 4.85 + 0.15 = 5.00

19 0.947 0.972 0.989 1.027 1.029 Zero point something is less than 1 point something. So 0.947, 0.989, and 0.972 come before 1.029 and 1.027. Then look at the tenths column first with the numbers starting with zero: 0.947, 0.989, 0.972; 7 is less than 8 so the order of these is 0.947, 0.972, 0.989. With the numbers starting with 1, the digits in the tenths and hundredths columns are the same, so look at the next column (thousandths): 1.029 1.027 and 9 is greater than 7. The final order is 0.947 0.972 0.989 1.027 1.029.

20 In each of these decimal numbers there are 5 or more tenths, so they all round up to the next whole number.
   a 58   57.56
   b 410   409.64
   c 1100   1099.91

21 When rounding to 1 decimal place inspect the number in the hundredths column:
   a 4.7   4.673
   b 73.8   73.849
   c 30.0   29.958
   Even if there is zero in the tenths column it needs to be written in as the question asks for answers correct to 1 decimal place.

22 All 3 answers in a row must be correct for 1 mark

		Divided by 100	Divided by 10	Divided by 1000
a	1257.3	12.573	125.73	1.2573
b	90.83	0.9083	9.083	0.09083
c	484.9	4.849	48.49	0.4849

23 3.157 It is more than 3.15 and less than 3.16. The step from 3.15 and 3.16 is divided into 10 small squares with the arrow pointing to the 7, so the number is 3.157.

24 150 The calculation is $\frac{60}{100} \times 250$, cancelling it down goes to $\frac{6}{10} \times 250$ which goes to $6 \times 25 = 120$

25 ($1\frac{1}{2}$ marks each)
   a £68.20 Bought for (£22 + £30 + £10) = £62; 10% of £62 = £6.20, so he sells for £62+ £6.20 = £68.20
   b £11.80 The extra profit is £80 –£68.20 = £11.80

26 80p $\frac{20}{100} \times £4 = \frac{1}{5} \times 400p = 80p$

27 a £2.10 75% = $\frac{3}{4}$; $\frac{3}{4} \times £1.20 = 90p$; so the increased price is £1.20 = 90p = £2.10
   b £2.25 25% = $\frac{1}{4}$; $\frac{1}{4} \times £3.00 = 75p$; so the reduced price is £3.00 – 75p = £2.25

28 a 112 40% = $\frac{4}{10} = \frac{2}{5}$; if $\frac{1}{5}$ of 280 is 56, then $\frac{2}{5}$ is $56 \times 2 = 112$
   b 315 70% = $\frac{7}{10}$; if $\frac{1}{10}$ of 450 is 45, then $\frac{7}{10}$ is $7 \times 45 = 315$

29 186.6 $373.2 \div 2 = 186.6$

30 a 30% Pizza is $\frac{3}{5}$ = 60%; burgers are 10%; so pasta is 100% – 60% – 10% = 30%
   b 6 10% of 20 is 2, so 30% of 20 = 6

31 $\frac{7}{8}$ $\frac{3}{5} = \frac{6}{10}$; 60% = $\frac{6}{10}$; 0.6 = $\frac{6}{10}$; $\frac{7}{8}$ does not equal a whole number of tenths; $\frac{6}{10}$; so $\frac{7}{8}$ is the odd one out. All the others are the equivalent of $\frac{6}{10}$; $\frac{3}{5} = \frac{6}{10}$ when both numbers are multiplied by 2; 60% = $\frac{60}{100}$ which simplifies to $\frac{6}{10}$; 0.6 = $\frac{6}{10}$

32 0.03, 3% Convert the decimals and percentages to fractions: 0.3 = $\frac{30}{100}$; 0.03 = $\frac{3}{100}$; 0.003 = $\frac{3}{1000}$; 3% = $\frac{3}{100}$ which shows that 0.03 and 3% are the same as $\frac{3}{100}$.

33 **0.07, 7%** Convert the decimals and percentages to fractions: **0.07** = $\frac{7}{100}$; 77% = $\frac{77}{100}$; 7% = $\frac{7}{100}$; 0.7 = $\frac{7}{10}$

34 Change the amounts shown to fractions with a denominator of 100 wherever possible: $\frac{6}{10} = \frac{60}{100}$; 40% = $\frac{40}{100}$; $\frac{4}{5} = \frac{80}{100}$; 0.8 = $\frac{80}{100}$; $\frac{4}{7}$ cannot be changed like this cannot be answer; $\frac{4}{5}$ and 0.8 are both equivalents of $\frac{80}{100}$

Learning Paper 4: Algebra and codes

1 **3** $7a = 21$; $a = 21 \div 7 = 3$
2 **7** $12x = 84$; $x = 84 \div 12 = 7$
3 **15** $60 = 4y$; $60 \div 4 = y = 15$
4 a **31** $7 \times 5 = 35$; $35 - 4 = 31$
   b **38** $10 + 25 = 35$; $35 + 3 = 38$
5 **9** $3y - 7 = 20$; $3y = 20 + 7 = 27$; $y = 27 \div 3 = 9$
6 **23** $14 + 9 = 23$
7 **28** $3c = 15$; $2a = 4$; $3b = 9$; $15 + 4 + 9 = 28$
8 **47** $2x = 20$; $3y = 15$; $z = 12$; $20 + 15 + 12 = 47$
9 **21**
10 **5, 10, 15**
11 **35** $a^2 = 5 \times 5 = 25$; $25 + 10 = 35$
12 **c** The first letter represents the position of the small square within the larger square (A is at the top left corner, B is at the top right corner, C is at the bottom left corner); the second letter represents the style of shading (X is diagonal lines, Y is grid lines, Z is black).
13 **a** The first letter represents the number of small circles along the outer edge of 1 side (A is 2, B is 3, C is 4). The second letter represents the position of the large white circle (X is inside the triangle, Y is crossing 1 edge of the triangle, Z is across 1 corner of the triangle).
14 **d** The first letter is the orientation of the zigzag line (D is as a 'Z', E is as an 'N', F is as a back-to-front 'N'). The second letter represents the number of loops on the curved line (L is 1, M is 2, N is 3).
15 **c** The first letter represents the position of the small circle inside the large circle (A is at the top, B is to the right, C is at the bottom). The second letter represents the shading of the small circle (X is black, Y is white, Z has a cross).
16 **b** The first letter represents the shading of the oval shape (A is white, B is black, C has line shading). The second letter represents the number of short lines crossing the long line (X is 1, Y is 2, Z is 3).
17 **c** The first letter represents the shape inside the square (A is a square, B is a circle, C is a triangle). The second letter represents the shading style (X is white, Y is lines, Z is black).
18 **c** The first letter represents the orientation of the zigzag line (D is as a 'Z', E is as a back-to-front 'Z', F is as an 'N'). The second letter represents the number of horizontal lines at the base of the shape (R is 1, S is 2, T is 3).
19 **e** The first letter represents the shape along the curved line (L is for diamonds, M is for circles, N is for triangles). The second letter represents the number of shapes (A is 3, B is 4, C is 5).

20 **b** The first letter represents the shape (E is a square, F is a diamond, G is a trapezium). The second letter represents the line pattern (A is a single dashed line, B is double plain lines, C is inner line dashed with outer plain line, D is a single plain line).
21 **71** $7a = 49$, $100 - 49 = 51$, $51 + 20 = 71$
22 **88** $940 \div 5 = 188$; $10^2 = 100$; $188 - 100 = 88$
23 **8** $\frac{1}{2} \times 64 = 32$, $32 + 8 = 40$
24 **11** $10y = 70$, $70 \div 5 = 14$, $14 - 3 = 11$
25 **234** $690 \div 3 = 230$, $230 + 4 = 234$
26 **21** $152 \div 4 = 38$, $38 - 17 = 21$
27 **120** $45 \times 2 = 90$; $150 \div 5 = 30$; $90 + 30 = 120$
28 **94** $156 \div 12 = 13$; $27 \times 3 = 81$; $13 + 81 = 94$
29 **22** $3^2 = 3 \times 3 = 9$; $91 \div 7 = 13$, $9 + 13 = 22$
30 **4** $4^2 = 16$, $16 + 24 = 40$; $3^2 = 9$, $9 + 1 = 10$; $40 \div 10 = 4$
31 **37** $3a = 3 \times 5 = 15$, $15 \times 2 = 30$, $30 + 7 = 37$
32 **19** $4z = 16$, $16 + 3 = 19$; $3y = 9$, $9 - 2 = 7$; $3x = 6$, $6 + 1 = 7$; so $19 + 7 - 7 = 19$
33 **20** $\frac{32}{4} = 8$; $3 \times 4 = 12$; $8 + 12 = 20$

Learning Paper 5: Shape, Space and Nets

1 **6** The 2 hexagonal faces, 1 at each end of the prism, are joined by rectangular faces, 1 from each edge of the hexagon.
2 a **square-based pyramid**
3 a **cuboid**
   b **triangular-based pyramid or tetrahedron**
   c **cylinder**
4 **8**
5 **b** and **d** A regular polygon has all sides the same length and all interior angles the same size.
6 a **kite** Adjacent pairs of sides of equal length.
   b **trapezium** One pair of parallel sides.
   c **rhombus** All sides of equal length and opposite sides are parallel.
7 **90°** (or a right angle) ⌚
8 **135°** North to east is 90°, east to south east is $\frac{1}{2} \times 90° = 45°$, $90° + 45° = 135°$
9

	35°	120°	60°	240°
Acute angle	x		x	
Obtuse angle		x		
Reflex angle				x

An acute angle is >0 and <90°; an obtuse angle is >90° and <180°, and a reflex angle is >180°.
10 **a** and **d** Both are more than 90° and less than 180°.
11 a **270°** $90° + 90° + 90° = 270°$
   b **reflex angle**
12 **18°** Angles around a point add up to 360°; $93 + 84 + 165 = 342$, $360 - 342 = 18$
13 **111°** Angles on a straight line add up to 180°; $45 + 24 = 69$, $180 - 69 = 111$
14 **360°** The internal angles in any quadrilateral add up to 360°.

15 **c** All of the shapes apart from c have the arrow coming out from the middle of the shape at the top.

16 **d** All of the shapes apart from d have a short straight line linking the square and the circle.

17 **d** All of the shapes apart from d have only flat faces, no curved faces.

18 **d** All of the shapes apart from d have elements in threes.

19 **a** All of the shapes on the left are enclosed shapes made up of 4 straight lines.

20 **d** All of the shapes on the left have 4 sections with 1 section shaded black.

21 **e** All of the shapes on the left are made up of a plain line and a dotted line, with the plain line on the outside when the shape is closed.

22 **b** All of the shapes on the left are made up of 3 lines.

23 **e** All of the shapes on the left are quadrilaterals.

24 **a** of the shapes on the left have a line protruding out of a corner of the square, and a smaller shape in or on the opposite corner.

25 **c** All of the shapes on the left are made up of 3 lines or shapes.

26 **d** All of the shapes on the left are made up of 2 overlapping shapes with their intersection shaded with diagonal lines.

27 **d** It cannot be cube a as the black dots should be on opposite sides, or cube c as the squares should be on opposite sides. It cannot be cube b as there is no completely shaded face on the net. It cannot be cube e as the cross and white circle should be on opposite sides.

28 **c** It cannot be cube a as the triangle should be next to the black part of the face with a black and white rectangle. It cannot be cube b as the black semicircle and white circle should be on opposite sides. It cannot be cubes d or e as the black semicircle should be above the triangle.

29 **e** It cannot be cube a as the face with the white circle should show a single dot. It cannot be cube b as the orientation of the three dots should be the same as the two dots on the front face. It cannot be cube c as the face with two dots will always be opposite one of the white circles. It cannot be cube d as two dots should be on the top face.

30 **a** It cannot be cube a as the face with the white circle should show a single dot. It cannot be cube b as the orientation of the three dots should be the same as the two dots on the front face. It cannot be cube c as the face with two dots will always be opposite one of the white circles. It cannot be cube d as two dots should be on the top face.

Learning Paper 6: Position and direction

1 **south-east** 45 degrees clockwise from north is north-east; 90 degrees clockwise from north-east is south-east.

2
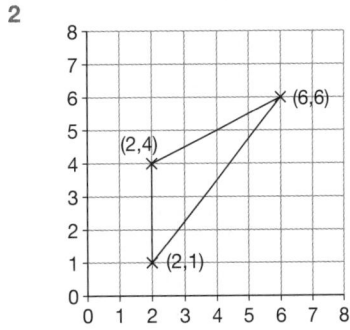

A triangle in which all 3 sides are a different length is called **scalene**.

3 **south** 90° clockwise from east is south.

4 **A (−3,1), B (1,4), C (5,2)** Give the number along the x axis first.

5 **(1,3)** All points where $y = 3$ will be on this line.

6 **(2,4)**
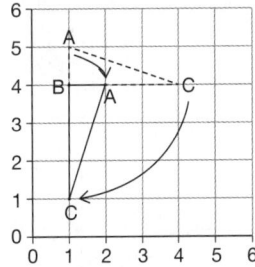

7
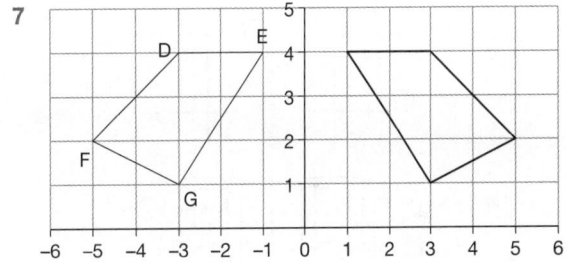

8
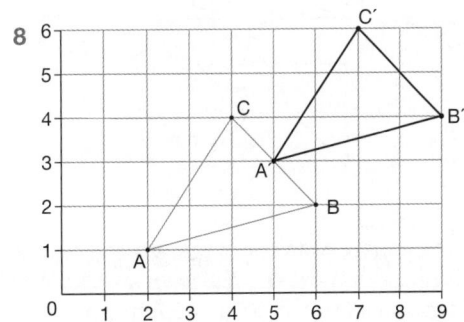

The number for the x axis increases by 3 and the number for the y axis increases by 2; therefore the new coordinates are A = (5, 3) B = (9, 4) C = (7, 6)

9
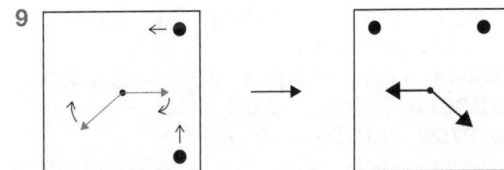

10 c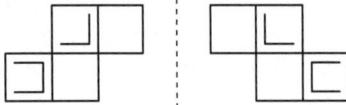

11 e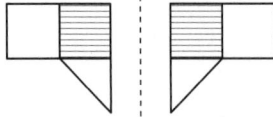

12 b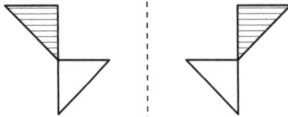

13 d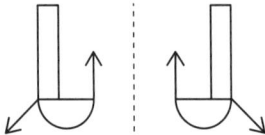

14 a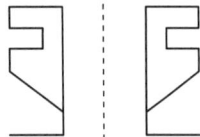

15 d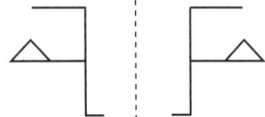

16 c

17 b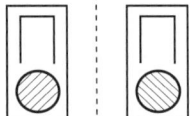

18 e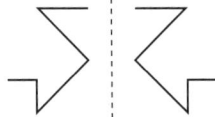

Learning Paper 7: Measurement and Pairs

1 **600 cm** 2 m = 200 cm; 0.5 m = 50 cm; so 200 + 350 + 50 = 600 cm

2 **3030 ml** There are 1000 ml in a litre so 3.03 × 1000 = 3030

3 a **4200 ml** 4.2 × 1000 = 4200
   b **0.47 kg** There are 1000 g in a kg, so 470 ÷ 1000 = 0.47

4 **4500 m** 1 km = 1000 m, so 4.5 × 1000 = 4500

5 **72.35 km** 72 350 ÷ 1000 = 72.35

6 a **07:20** b **15:30** c **21:15**
   To change times shown in a.m. to 24-hour clock, use the same digits and insert a zero before the hour if only 3 digits are shown. To change p.m. time, add 12 to the hours between 1 p.m. and 11 p.m.

7 a **4.25 a.m.** b **1.20 p.m.** c **7.10 p.m.**
   To change times shown in 24-hour clock to analogue, if the time shown is between 00:00 and 11:59, write the same digits and add a.m., removing the zero from the front if needed. 12:00 onwards is p.m., so if the time shown is between 13:00 and 23:59, subtract 12 from the hours and add p.m.

8 **15.4 lbs** 7 × 2.2 = 15.4 lbs

9 **13 feet** 39 × 4 = 156 inches, divide by 12 to convert inches to feet: 156 ÷ 12 = 13 feet

10 **14 cm** A hexagon has 6 sides and 84 ÷ 6 sides = 14

11 **648 m** The perimeter of the paddock is 55 + 55 + 110 + 110 = 330 m; 2 strands all round = 660 m; less 12 m as there are no strands across the two 3 m wide gates: 660 − 12 = 648

12 **11 cm** The short sides = 2 + 2 = 4 cm; total of the long sides = 26 − 4 = 22 cm, so each long side is 22 ÷ 2 = 11 cm

13 **4.5 cm²** The area of the square is 3 × 3 = 9 cm², so the area of triangle is 9 ÷ 2 = 4.5 cm²

14 **3 cm** Area = length × width, so width = area ÷ length = 75 ÷ 25 = 3 cm

15 **1000 cm³** Volume is length × width × height which for a 10 cm cube is 10 × 10 × 10 = 1000 cm³

16 **320 cm³** Volume of the box is 10 × 4 × 8 = 320 cm³

17 **1 000 000 cubic centimetres** Volume of a metre cube in cm³ = 100 × 100 × 100 = 1 000 000

18 **10 cm³** There are ten 1 cm³ cubes and 10 × 1 cm³ = 10 cm³

19 **16:04** 15:47 to 16:00 is 13 minutes; 17 − 13 = 4 so there are still 4 mins to add: 16:00 + 4 mins = 16:04

20 a **10:59** 10: 16 to 10: 35 = 19 mins and 10:40 + 19 min = 10.59
   b **4 mins** 10:16 to 11:06 = 50 minutes for the 1st train; 10:40 to 11:30 = 50 minutes for the 2nd train; 11:04 to 11:50 = 46 minutes for the 3rd train; 50-46 = 4 minutes
   c **11:43** total delay between A and D is 17 − 4 = 13 mins, so the second train will arrive at D at 11:30 + 00:13 = 11:43

21 **5 h 10 min 30 sec** 310.5 mins ÷ 60 for hours = 5 hours with a remainder of 10.5 mins which is 10 mins and 30 secs.

22 **Bus C** A is 08:40 − 08:20 = 20 mins, B is 08:58 − 08:30 = 28 mins, C is 09:48 − 09:30 = 18 mins; the quickest journey will be the shortest time.

23 e The second pattern has the top shape moved into the square and the shape inside the square moved below the bottom edge of the square. The shape at the bottom left of the square is rotated 180° around the outside.

24 c The second pattern is 2 copies of the first pattern, 1 above the other.

25 c The second shape is the first shape rotated 180° with an additional line in bold at the bottom.

26 d The second shape is the first shape rotated 90 degrees clockwise.

27 a The second shape is a triangle with the same shading as the top left quarter of the square.

28 d The second shape has the same number of sides as there are short lines in the first shape, and that same number of circles repeated inside the shape.

1 a **20** 42 on Sunday, 22 on Thursday, the difference is $42 - 22 = 20$

   b **141** Friday 51, Saturday 48, Sunday 42, total for the 3 days is $51 + 48 + 42 = 141$

   c **30** Tuesday had 24, 25% of 24 = 6, so with an increase of 6, the new total will be $24 + 6 = 30$

2 a

   b **u**   c **e**

   d **200** total is $45 + 55 + 45 + 35 + 20 = 200$

   e **10%** $\frac{20}{200} = \frac{10}{100} = 10\%$

3 a **24°C**

   b **7°C** 22°C at 16:00, 15°C at 20:00; the difference is $22 - 15 = 7°C$

   c **7 hours** 11:00 = 23°C;12:00 = 24°C; 13:00 = 24°C; 14:00 = 25°C; 15:00 = 23°C; 16:00 = 22°C; and 17:00 = 21°C

4 a **4°C**

   b **16°C** 9:00 a.m. to 11.30 a.m. is $2\frac{1}{2}$ hrs, so count on $2\frac{1}{2}$ squares from the first hour: the line meets the y axis at 16°C

   c from **2.00 p.m. to 3.00 p.m.** The highest temperature shown is 19°C which is between 5 and 6 hours after the first time shown at 9.00 a.m.; 9.00 a.m. + 5 hrs = 2.00 p.m. and 9.00 a.m. + 6 hrs = 3.00 p.m. (Also accept 14:00 to 15:00)

5 a **7** Add together the numbers that are in both the 'cat' circle and the 'dog' circle, $4 + 3 = 7$

   b **4** Add together all of the numbers recorded in the Venn diagram as they all have at least 1 pet: $7 + 4 + 8 + 3 + 1 + 3 = 26$, so number of children with no pet is $30 - 26 = 4$

6 **Cheese** Cheese is $10 + 7 + 4 + 2 = 23$; pineapple is $10 + 3 + 2 + 6 = 21$; mushroom is $2 + 6 + 4 + 5 = 17$

7 **September**

Temp in °C	Jan	Feb	Mar	Apr	May	Jun	Jul	Aug	Sep	Oct	Nov	Dec
Min	−6	−4	2	6	9	10	10	9	6	3	3	−2
Max	8	9	12	17	21	24	26	27	25	21	16	10
Difference	14	13	14	11	12	14	16	18	**19**	18	13	12

8 **8 months** Apr, May, Jun, Jul, Aug, Sep, Oct, Nov

9 Between **Oct and Nov**

Difference	14	13	14	11	12	14	16	18	**19**	18	13	12
	1	1	3	1	2	2	2	1	**1**	5	1	2

10 **1** Hockey is $5 \times 5 = 25$; tennis is $8 \times 3 = 24$; $25 - 24 = 1$

Curveball Questions 1

1 **Some mammals eat meat.** Consider each statement in turn. 'All mammals eat meat' – no, the statement only says that lions eat meat. 'Some mammals eat meat' – yes, the statement says that lions are mammals and they eat meat. 'Some lions are mammals' – no, the statement says that all lions are mammals. 'All mammals are lions' – no, the statement says that lions are mammals.

2 **13** $\frac{1}{3}$ of total counters are green and there are 20 green counters. So if $\frac{1}{3}$ is 20, the total is $20 \times 3 = 60$. Of the 40 counters that are not green there is 1 yellow, so 39 are red or blue. Share 39 into 3 equal parts so that red counters account for $\frac{2}{3}$ and blue $\frac{1}{3}$. So the blue counters amount to $\frac{1}{3} \times 39 = 13$

3 94153   79143   51937   93173

   DATES   TEASE   STARE   TRADE

4 a Start with the rows of columns that have 2 numbers already inserted: $5 + 3 = 8$ and $15 - 8 = \mathbf{7}$; $3 + 4 = 7$ and $15 - 7 = 8$; $1 + \mathbf{8} = 9$ and $15 - 9 = \mathbf{6}$; $5 + 1 = 6$ and $15 - 6 = \mathbf{9}$; $9 + 4 = 13$ and $15 - 13 = \mathbf{2}$

5	7	3
9	2	4
1	6	8

15

   b $8 + 5 = 13$ and $20 - 13 = \mathbf{7}$; $8 + 7 = 15$ and $20 - 15 = \mathbf{5}$: $10 + 5 = 15$ and $20 - 15 = \mathbf{5}$; $5 + 8 = 13$ and $20 - 13 = \mathbf{7}$; $7 + 8 = 15$ and $20 - 15 = \mathbf{5}$

5	10	5
7	5	8
8	5	7

20

c 15 + 2 = 17 and 25 − 17 = **8**; 8 + 3 = 11 and
25 − 11 = **14**; 14 + 6 = 20 and 25 − 20 = **5**:
5 + 2 = 7 and 25 − 7 − **18**; 3 + 18 = 21 and
25 − 21 = **4**

14	6	5
3	4	18
8	15	2

25

d 10 + 8 = 18 and 30 − 18 = **12**; 13 + 10 = 23 and
30 − 23 = **7**; 14 + 7 = 21 and 30 − 21 = **9**; 9 + 8
= 17 and 30 − 17 = **13**; 13 + 13 = 26 and 30 −
26 = **4**

14	7	9
4	13	13
12	10	8

30

Mixed Paper 1

1 a **41**   26,   27,   29,   32,   36   …
      +1   +2   +3   +4   +5
The difference between the numbers increases
by 1 each time so 36 + 5 = 41

b **13**   65,   52,   39,   26   …
      −13   −13   −13   −13
The difference decreases by 13 each time; so
26 − 13 = 13

c **1408**   1004,   1105,   1206,   1307   …
      +101   +101   +101   +101
The difference increases by 101 each time so
1307 + 101 = 1408

d **256**   1,   4,   16,   64   …
      +3   +12   +48   +192
If there is no clear pattern from the differences,
look carefully at the numbers. In both the
sequence of numbers and the sequence of
differences, each term is the previous number
×4, so the next term is 64 × 4 = 256

2 **£4.25** A ticket for a child is £10.50 ÷ 2 = £5.25;
3 tickets are £5.25 × 3 = £15.75; the money left is
£20 − 15.75 = £4.25

3 **d** Circles are removed 1 by 1 from the right-hand
end of the pattern.

4 **b** A line is added to the right side of the shape
each tie, alternating between vertical and
horizontal.

5 **c** The triangles rotate 90 degrees clockwise
between each term and the shading follows the
pattern of horizontal lines, vertical lines, black.

6 **c** The '@', '!' and heart alternate with a sequence
of triangles; the triangles follow a pattern of
pointing up and down; the horizontal lines follow
a pattern of being above and below the shapes
each time.

7 **b** Black and white circles alternate; the number
of lines from the circles increases by 1 each time,
alternating between long and short lines.

8 **9 years** Read through the whole question first to
find the best place to start: Mrs Brown is 37 and
the middle child is 25 years younger (37 − 25 = 12
years); the eldest must be 14 as the middle child
is 2 years younger (12 + 2 = 14); the youngest
child must be 9 as they are 5 years younger than
the eldest (14 − 5 = 9)

9 **56 seconds** Ali is 7 seconds faster than Saqif,
and faster than Doug at 59 seconds. Ali is
10 seconds faster than Doug. Ben, at 47 seconds,
is 2 seconds faster than Ali. So Ali's time is 59 −
10 = 49 seconds. Ali, at 49 seconds, is 7 seconds
faster than Saqif, so Saqif's time is 49 + 7 =
56 seconds

10 $\frac{6}{9}$ $\frac{3}{10}$ 30% = $\frac{30}{100}$ = $\frac{3}{10}$ $\frac{9}{30}$ = $\frac{3}{10}$ $\frac{6}{9}$ = $\frac{2}{3}$

0.3 = $\frac{3}{10}$ All the amounts shown can be simplified

to or converted to $\frac{3}{10}$.

11 **454.6 cm** 4.2 m = 420 cm; 16 mm = 1.6 cm;
420 + 33 + 1.6 = 454.6

12 a **26 m** Find the lengths of the missing sides:
8 − 4 = 4 and 3 + 2 = 5; then add all the lengths
together (8 + 3 + 4 + 2 + 4 + 5 = 26)

b **8 sq m** The area of garden is (8 m × 5 m)-
(2 m × 4 m) = 40 − 8 = 32 sq m; the patio is
one-quarter of the area, which is $\frac{1}{4}$ × 32 =
8 sq m.

13 a **20%**

b **12** 60% of 20 is $\frac{60}{100}$ × 20 = 12

c **7** 70% have dogs so 355 have cats and dogs;
$\frac{35}{100}$ × 20 = 7

d **1** 5% which is $\frac{30}{100}$ × 20 = 1

14 **6**   53 721.046 2 + 4 = 6

15 **3**   8   10   **13**   **29**   42

16 **125** 5^3 = 5 × 5 × 5 = 125

17 **4** Red = $\frac{1}{2}$ × 80 = 40; yellow = $\frac{1}{4}$ × 80 = 20; green

is $\frac{1}{5}$ × 80 = 16; orange is 80 − (40 + 20 + 16) = 4

18 **79** (4 × 6) + (69 − 14) = 24 + 55 = 79

19 **449** 584 − (45 × 3) = 584 − 135 = 449

20 **92** (5^2 + 6^2) + (217 ÷ 7) = (25 + 36) + 31 = 92

21 **1150 ml** 400 ml +25 ml = 425 ml, so in each litre:
1000 ml − 425 ml of soda = 575 ml. To make
2 litres there needs to be 575 ml × 2 = 1150 ml

22 **40 000 cm** 1 m = 100 cm, 0.5 m = 50 cm and 0.8
cm = 80 cm; 100 x 50 = 5000 and 5000 x 80
= 40 000 cm

23 **BR** The first letter represents the shading of
the circle in the bottom left square (A is black,
B is white, C has a cross). The second letter
represents the direction of the arrow in the top
right square (R points to the right, S points up,
T points down).

24 **b** All of the shapes except b are made up of a
small curved shape with an arrow.

25 d

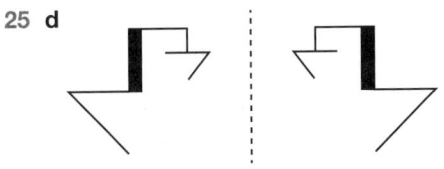

26 98° Interior angles of a quadrilateral add up to 360. The sum of the 3 interior angles is $57° + 85° + 120° = 262°$; the fourth angle is $360° - 262° = 98°$

27 124° The missing angle on the straight line is $180 - 110 = 70°$; interior angles = $70 + 81 + 85 = 236°$; so $x = 360° - 236° = 124°$

28 c A face with a black arrow has to have the arrow pointing to a face with a white circle.

29 A is (–4,1), B is (0,3), C is (4,2)

30 scalene

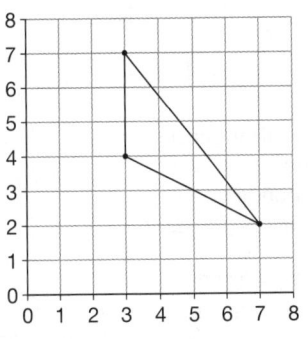

31

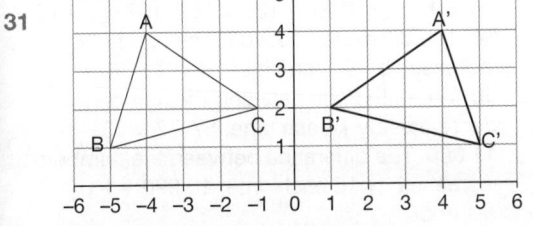

A' is (4,4). B' is (1,2), C' is (5,1)

Mixed Paper 2

1 24 All the other numbers are square numbers.

2 11 $67 + 22 = 89$; $100 - 89 = 11$

3 12 a 1, 5, 7, 35 (The number itself and 1 are always factors.)
  b *Any 4 of*: 1, 2, 4, 5, 10, 20
  c 1, 3, 11, 33

4 12 cm The short sides give $4 \times 2 = 8$, both long sides give $32 - 8 = 24$, 1 long side is $\frac{1}{2}$ of $24 = 12$

5 631 m Width = 80 m, length = 80 m $\times$ 3 = 240 m, perimeter is $(2 \times 80) + (2 \times 240) = 160 + 480 = 640$ m, less the width of three 3 m gates, $640 - 9 = 631$ m

6 a 5 litres $20\% + 20\% + 20\% = 60\%$; the whole drink is 100% so subtract to find the percentage of lemonade added ($100\% - 60\% = 40\%$ lemonade in 2 litres); convert to ml and find 10% by dividing by 4 ($2000 \div 4 = 500$ so 10% = 500 ml); then multiply by 10 to find 100% ($500 \times 10 = 5000$ ml, which is 5 litres)
  b 25 5 litres = 5000 ml, number of 200 ml glasses is $5000 \div 200 = 50 \div 2 = 25$

7 £11.03 $3 \times £1.20 = £3.60$, $3 \times 80p = £2.40$, $3 \times 99p = £2.97$, $£3.60 + £2.40 + £2.97 = £8.97$, $£20 - £8.97 = £11.03$

8 d All shapes are made up of 4 elements.

9 d All of the shapes on the left are enclosed, with straight sides and single plain lines.

10 e All of the shapes on the left have a small shape within a larger, different shape.

11 c All of the shapes on the left are L-shapes with right angles and with 1 line longer than the other.

12 b All of the shapes on the left have the same number of black circles as loops along their line.

13 c The outer squares of the grid are mirror images of the opposite outer square, so the missing square is a reflection of the square on the right.

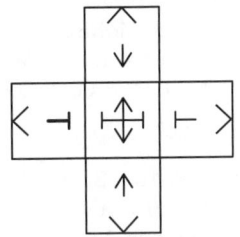

14 b Each row has the shapes in the same position, and the number of shapes in each square decreases down each column, so the missing square has a white circle in the top left corner.

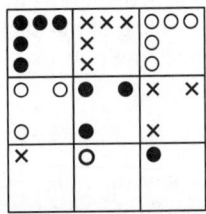

15 e In the lower row the vertical line progresses from left to right along the row.

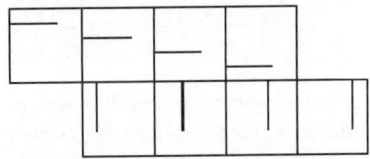

16 e The triangular quarters within the square are identical, giving a pattern of black and white circles alternating around the grid.

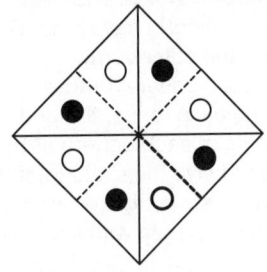

17 a 750 m The perimeter is $220 + 150 + 180 + 200 = 750$ m
  b 4 3 km = 3000 m, $3000 \div 750 = 4$ times

18 7 cm The candle is 3 cm shorter every hour, so 1 cm shorter every 20 minutes. So by 9.30 p.m. the candle is 11 cm; 10.10 p.m. is 40 minutes later so it is another 2 cm shorter, so the final height is 7 cm.

Bond CEM Maths & NVR Assessment Papers 9–10 years

19 a **44°C** Each division on the *y* axis represents 2°C.
   b Anything **between 90 seconds and 100 seconds**
20 a **638.9**
   b **639**
   c **600** When rounding, if the digit in the column to the right is 5 or more the number rounds up – for nearest tenth 638.**8**7 the 8 rounds up; for nearest whole number 63**8**.87 the 9 rounds up; for nearest hundred **6**38.87 the 6 does not round up.
21 a *Any 6 of* **2, 3, 4, 5, 6, 10, 12, 15, 20, 30** All divide exactly into 60.
   b **35** 47 54 **63** 81 In order to be a multiple of 7, the number must be exactly divisible by 7.
   c **Factor: any of 1, 2, 4, 8, 16. Multiple: 32 or 48**
22 **64** 24 is one-quarter of the journeys surveyed, so total number of journeys is 24 × 4 = 96; two-thirds arrived within 5 minutes, which is $\frac{2}{3}$ × 96 = 64
23 a **6** 35 – 17 = 18 so 3x = 18; 18 ÷ 3 = 6
   b **100** 640 ÷ 4 = 160; 160 – 60 = 100
   c **26** 4b = 32 (as 4 × 8 = 32) and 2a = 6 (as 2 × 3 = 6); 32 – 6 = 26
24 **4800 cubic cm** 40 × 12 = 480 and 480 × 10 = 4800
25 **10** There are 8 rectangles along the length of the prism and 2 flat octagonal faces, 1 at each end.
26 d Two faces with diagonal sets of 3 spots must fold to give the diagonals meeting at the same corner, which only occurs with net d.
27

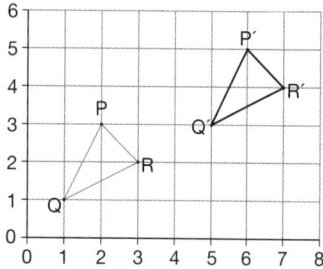

28 **RT** The first letter represents the direction of the arrow (P is down, Q is to the right, R is upward). The second letter represents the shading of the inner shape (S is black, T is white).

Mixed Paper 3

1 d The outer squares of the grid have a right-angled L-shape inside the outer corner.
2 c The pattern inside each square rotates clockwise by 90° along each row of the grid.
3 e The shaded elements of each pattern at the end of the rows combines to give the shading of the central pattern, so the missing triangle will have a smaller triangle at the top right with vertical line shading.
4 b The patterns in the outer squares of the grid are repeated in the inner square, so the missing square has 2 small white circles within it.
5 b

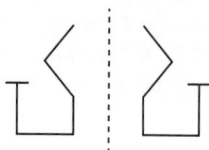

6 e

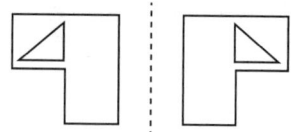

7 b

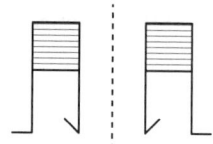

8 a

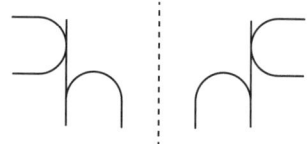

9 a **four hundred thousand**
   b **seven tenths**
10 a **770** 7**6**9.8 rounds up.
   b **990** 9**9**0.59 stays the same.
11 **3498**
12 **1529** 2000 – 471 = 1529
13 **108** 12^2 = 144, 6^2 = 36, 144 – 36 = 108
14 **151** 3^3 = 3 × 3 × 3 = 27; 5^3 = 5 × 5 × 5 = 125; 1^3 = 1 × 1 × 1 = 1; 27 + 125 = 152; 152 – 1 = 151
15 a **36** The difference between the numbers increases by 8 each time; 28 + 8 = 36
   b **50** The difference between the numbers decreases by 7 each time; 57 – 7 = 50
   c **11 000** The difference between the numbers increases by 10 each time; 10 990 + 10 = 11 000
16 $\frac{4}{5}$, $\frac{16}{24}$ Reduce fractions to lowest terms to compare them:
   $\frac{4}{6} = \frac{2}{3}$ $\frac{9}{10}$ $\frac{5}{15} = \frac{1}{3}$ $\frac{16}{24} = \frac{2}{3}$ $\frac{3}{15} = \frac{1}{5}$ $\frac{1}{6}$
17 a $\frac{1}{5}$ To reduce the fractions divide the numerator and denominator by the same number.
   b $\frac{2}{3}$
   c $\frac{7}{8}$
18 **£75** 15% of £500 = $\frac{15}{100}$ × 500 = 15 × 5 = £75
19 **20%** Reduction is £24 – £19.20 = £4.80; % reduction is $\frac{480}{2400}$ × 100 = $\frac{480}{24}$ = 20%
20 **12** 73 + 6x = 145, 6x = 145 – 73 = 72, so x = 12
21 **61** 10 × 10 = 100 so a2 = 100; 3 × 13 = 39 so 3b = 39; 100 – 39 = 61
22 **2.9 cm** Diameter is twice the radius, so radius is $\frac{1}{2}$ of 5.8 = 2.9 cm
23 **9** There are eight vertices around the octagonal base and 1 at the apex.

24

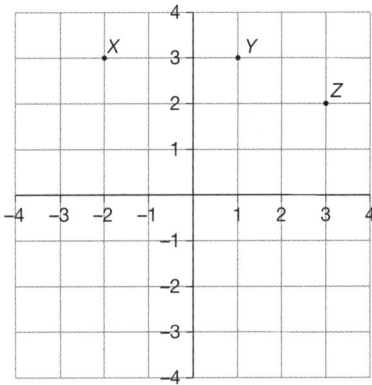

25 **(3,2)** Moving N moves up the y axis, the second digit in a coordinate relates to the y axis, so −5 + 7 = 2

26 **0.745** Divide by 10 for cm, then by 100 for metres: 745 mm = 74.5 cm = 0.745 m

27 **5250 g** 5 kg = 5 × 1000 g = 5000 g; $\frac{1}{4}$ × 1 kg = $\frac{1}{4}$ × 1000 g = 250 g; total is 5250 g

28 **6000 000** 1.5 cm = 150 cm; 150 x 50 = 7500; 7500 x 80 = 600 000

29 **200 cartons** 9l is 90 000 ml; 90 000 ÷ 450 = 200

30 **a** **21** 31 − 10 = 21

   b $\frac{1}{5}$ 24 + 31 + 20 + 15 + 10 = 100, l is $\frac{20}{100} = \frac{1}{5}$

   c **a 29, e 21, i 15, o 15, u 10** For e 31 − 10 = 21; for 1 20 − 5 = 15; for a 24 + 5 = 29, o and u are unchanged.

31 **6 days** 12 − 6 = 6

32

Oranges	☺	☺	☺	☺	☺		
Bananas	🍌	🍌	🍌	🍌			
Apples	🍎	🍎	🍎	🍎	🍎	🍎	🍎
Grapes	🍇	🍇	🍇	🍇	🍇	🍇	🍇

(Any shape or symbol can be used as long as it is consistent in a row.)

33 **a = 80°** Angles in a triangle add up to 180, so 50 = 50 = 100, 180 − 100 = 80
b = 130° Angles along a straight line add up to 180, so 180 − 50 = 130

34 **810°** One complete turn is 360°, so 2 turns is 720°; a quarter turn is 90°, so a total spin is 810°

Mixed Paper 4

1 **b** All of the shapes on the left have a smaller diagonally shaded shape within the larger shape.

2 **c** All of the shapes on the left have 5 straight-line edges.

3 **b** All of the shapes on the left are made up of 3 similar shapes linked together with two of the shapes shaded black.

4 **e** All of the circles on the left are shaded with 1 outer line and they are all the same size.

5 **13 013 013**

6 **15** 4702.483 So 7 + 8 = 15

7 **180.5**

8 **53** 409 − 56 = 53

9 *Any 4 of* **2, 4, 5, 10, 20, 25, 50**

10 *Any 3 of* **34, 51, 68, 85**

11 **d** An arrow needs to point to a face with a white circle and have the face with the black spot adjacent, which only occurs in net d. In a and b the arrows point away from the white circle, and in **c** the white circle will not be adjacent to the black spot.

12 **b** Two faces with diagonal rows of 3 dots must have the diagonals meeting at a corner, so not a or c. In d they will have a face with a cross on the top rather than the white circle.

13 **e** A plain straight arrow and a black-headed straight arrow point to the same point on the same edge, which only occurs in option e.

14 **c** Net a will have a triangle on the top face, option **b** will have a cross at the top, option d will have a black circle at the top, and option e will not have the circle faces adjacent.

15 **a** **70** 790 + 140 = 930; 1000 − 930 = 70
   b **109** 499 + 392 = 891; 1000 − 891 = 109
   c **923** 67 + 10 = 77; 1000 − 77 = 923

16 **6 seconds** Kelly = Annie + 5 secs; Jen = Annie + 11 secs, so the difference between Kelly and Jen is 6 seconds.

17 **The yellow car** Read through the whole question to find the best place to start: the yellow car is faster than the green car, which is faster than the red car; the grey car is faster than the red one but slower than the green one; as the red car was slower than the grey and green cars but faster than the blue car, the order must be: yellow, green, grey, red, blue.

18 **a** **20%** Half is 50%, one-fifth is 20%, one-tenth is 10%. So 100 − (50 + 20 + 10) = 20
   b **50** 20% of 250 = 20/100 × 250 = 50

19 **90** 10^2 − (3 × 6) + (48 ÷ 6) = 100 − 18 + 8 = 90

20 **32** 3^3 − 2^3 + (39 ÷ 3) = (3 × 3 × 3) − (2 × 2 × 2) + 13 = 27 − 8+13 = 32

21 **a** **45** Angles in a triangle add up to 180 so x = 180 − 90 − 45 = 45
   b **135** Angles on a straight line add up to 180 so y = 180 − 45 = 135

22 **P (−2,1), Q (2,2), R (1,−2), S (−3,−2)**

23 **a** **30 m** of fencing Calculate the missing measurements by looking at the opposite sides: 10 + 3 + 5 + 2 + 5 + 5 = 30
   b **Patio is 10 square metres** The area of the garden is (10 m × 5 m) − (5 m × 2 m) which is 50 m − 10 m = 40 m; divide by 4 to find $\frac{1}{4}$ (40 ÷ 4 = 10)

24 **22 cubic cm**

25 **24 cm³** Box A is 3 cm³ × 6 cm³ × 8 cm³ = 144 cm³ Box B is 4 cm³ × 5 cm³ × 6 cm³ = 120 cm³; difference is 144 cm³ − 120 cm³ = 24 cm³

26 **a** **16** 6 + 5 + 4 + 1 = 16
   b **13** 7 + 5 + 1 = 13

27 **a** **3**
   b **18**

28 **a** $\frac{41}{50}$ 82% = $\frac{82}{100} = \frac{41}{50}$
   b **0.82**

29 **a** **0.75**
   b **0.35** $\frac{7}{20} = \frac{35}{100}$

30 $\frac{7}{8}$ Convert all to have the same denominator: $\frac{1}{2} = \frac{4}{8}$; $\frac{1}{4} = \frac{2}{8}$; then add the numerators: $\frac{4}{8} + \frac{2}{8} + \frac{1}{8} = \frac{7}{8}$

Curveball Questions 2

References of the squares where there are differences between the 2 patterns:
B8, B10, C6, C11, D11, E6, F3, G1, I4, I5, J7, J11, K10, L10, M1, M2, M7, M10

Test Paper 1

1 a 41, 51

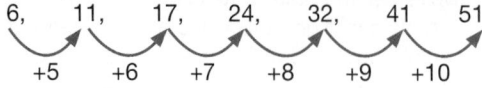

6,   11,   17,   24,   32,   41   51

+5   +6   +7   +8   +9   +10

b 64, 49

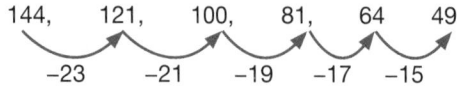

144,   121,   100,   81,   64   49

−23   −21   −19   −17   −15

c 310, 330

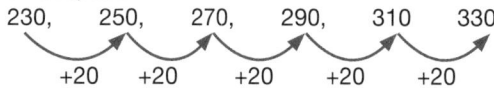

230,   250,   270,   290,   310   330

+20   +20   +20   +20   +20

2

6	4	10
1	11	8
13	5	2

3 a 27°C Boiling point is 100°C and the line crosses the y axis at 27°C

  b 12°C (11°C is an acceptable answer) The temperature on the y axis increases in 20s and there are 4 small squares between each temperature shown; 20 ÷ 4 = 5, so each small square represents 5°

  c The temperature on the y axis increases in 20s and there are 4 small squares between each temperature shown; 20 ÷ 4 = 5, so each small square represents 5°

4 e The small square stays in the same corner of the squares along the row; the circles stay in the same corner with alternating shading.

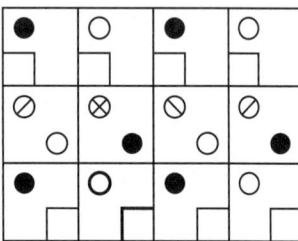

5 c The small square stays in the same position in the larger square for 2 consecutive patterns; the X rotates clockwise around the squares along each row.

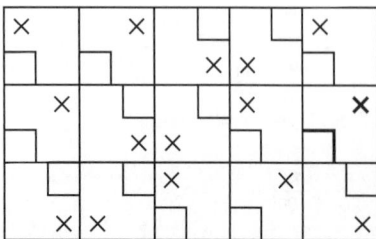

6 e The white shapes in the outer squares are repeated in the diagonally adjoining inner square, they are shaded in the same way as the shape in the adjacent outer square.

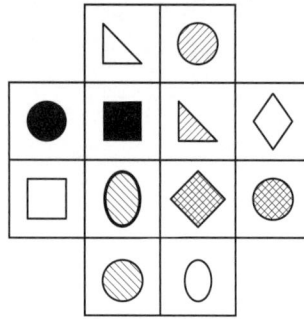

7 c The sequence follows left to right then down to the next row; the triangles alternate between pointing up and pointing down, and the shading follows the sequence: cross lines – white – black - diagonal lines.

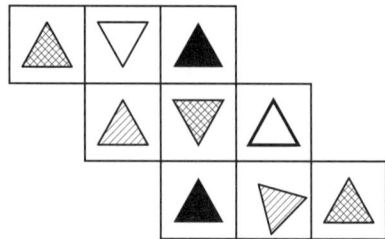

8 c All of the shapes on the right have 5 straight sides and 1 small black shape inside them.

9 b All of the arrows on the right have 3 lines of equal length.

10 d All of the patterns on the right have 3 black circles within them.

11 e All of the shapes on the right have 2 arrows with both arrowheads ending up inside or both outside of the circle.

12 c

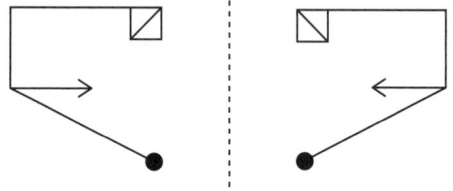

13 d

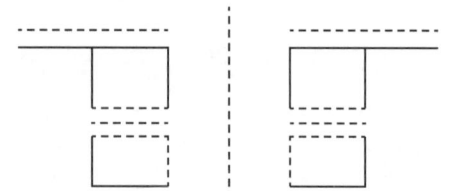

14 b

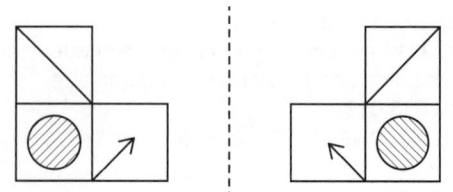

15 e

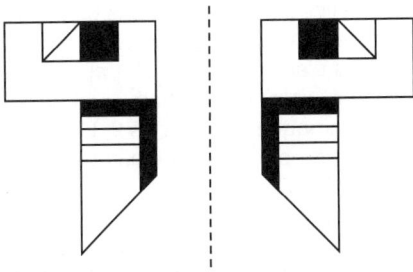

16 **Four hundred and one thousand, and sixty-seven point five**

17 **1303.13**

18 **46 335**

19 **45**

20 **219** 640–421 = 219

21 *Any 2 of* **12, 24, 36, 48** For a number to be a factor it must divide exactly into the number with no remainder.

22 **32, 52, 68** If a number is a multiple of 4 it can be divided by 4 exactly.

23 **c** The number of circles increases by 1 each time, alternating with black and white at the end, and the number of short lines behind the arrowhead decreases by 1 each time.

24 **e** The small white square is on alternate sides of the outer edge along the row, and the bottom right corner of the top squares and the top left corner of the lower squares have the same pattern diagonally opposite each other.

25 **d** The black squares move up to the top then down again along the sequence and the horizontal lines moves progressively down the rectangles.

26 **c** The lower part of the arrow rotates clockwise 45° each time and the arrow heads alternate between a V shape and a straight line.

27 **40** $\frac{1}{2}$ of 320 = 160; $\frac{1}{4}$ of 160 = 40

28 **£8.85** £2.50 + 45p = £2.95; as this is one third of her money, multiply by 3 to find the whole amount: £2.95 × 3 = £8.85

29 **15.82** 63.28 ÷ 4 = 15.82

30 $\frac{4}{5} = \frac{16}{20} = \frac{40}{50}$

31 a $\frac{3}{4}$

   b $\frac{5}{7}$

   c $\frac{3}{7}$

32 **17** 8 + 3 + 6 = 17

33 **7757.63**

34

decimal	fraction	%
0.7	$\frac{7}{10}$	**70%**
0.32	$\frac{8}{25}$	32%
0.6	$\frac{3}{5}$	**60%**

35 **11** Substituting gives (5 × 5) – (2 × 7) = 25 – 14 = 11

36 **8** If 7x + 17 = 73, then 7x = 73 – 17 = 56, so x = 56 ÷ 7 = 8

37 **55** (6 × 7) + (4² – 3) = 42 + (16 – 3) = 42 + 13 = 55

38 **95** 102 – (56 ÷8) = 102 – 7 = 95

39 **49** 5³ + 7² – 3³ = (5 × 5 × 5) + (7 × 7) – (3 × 3 × 3) = 125 + 49 – 27 = 49

40 **Cylinder**

41 **parallelogram** (rhombus will be accepted)

42 **59°**

43 **x is 48°** (180° – 132° = 48°); **y is 42°** (90° – 48° = 42)

44 **67°** 180° – 46° = 134°, base angles are equal so each angle is 134° ÷ 2 = 67°

45

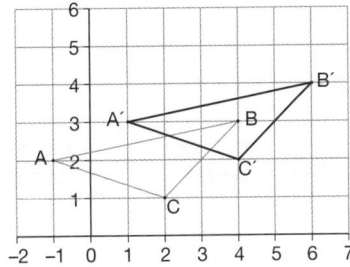

46 **225°** 180° + 45° = 225°

47

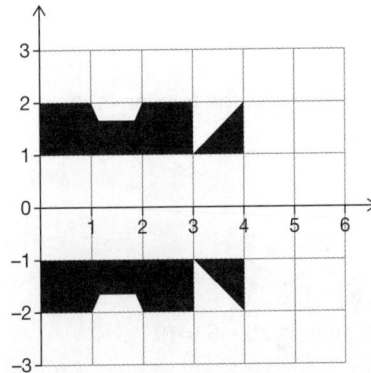

48 **36 cm** 4.5 cm × 8 = 36 cm

49 a **8 sq metres** The flower beds are 2 × 1 + 1 × 2 + 2 × 2 = 2 + 2 + 4 = 8 sq metres

   b **24 sq metres** The lawn area = (8 × 5) – (cut out of 4 × 2) – borders of 8 = 40 – 8 – 8 = 24

50 **880 m** Perimeter = (85 × 2) + (25 × 2) metres = 170 + 50 = 220 m, 4 rounds is 220 × 4 = 880 m

51 **3000 cm cubes** 50 × 12 × 5 = 50 × 60 = 3000

52 **0.5 m** 4 × 0.5 × ? = 1.0, volume is 1 cubic metre, then height is 0.5 m.

53 **8.07 p.m.** 8.23 p.m. – 12 minutes delay = 8.11 p.m., less 4 minutes late start = 8.07 p.m.

54 a **02:20**

   b **13:45**

   c **21:05**

55 a **72** 20 + 12 + 10 + 16 + 14 = 72

   b **A and D**

56

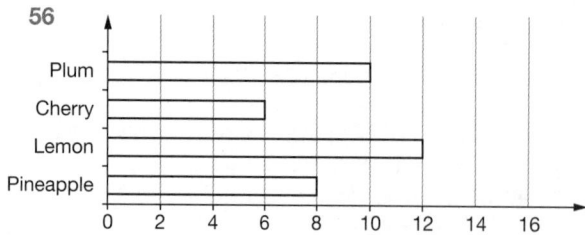

57 a **39 mm** 15 mm + 24 mm = 39 mm
b **Monday**
58 a **26** The total of the numbers within the swimming circle 2 + 10 + 6 + 8 = 26
b **21** The total of the numbers that are set inside just 1 of the 3 circles 7 + 10 + 4 = 21
59 a **10** The number in the section where all 3 circles overlap.
b **21** The total of the numbers within the 'blue' circle 10 + 6 + 3 + 2 = 21
60

	Chose cheese sandwich	Did not choose cheese sandwich
Chose orange juice	12	12
Did not choose orange juice	5	1

61 $\frac{2}{3}$ The total number is 8 + 12 + 6 + 4 = 30; in the choir are 8 + 12 = 20; the fraction in the choir is $\frac{20}{30} = \frac{2}{3}$

62 **19**

46   37   28   ?

–9   –9   –9

So the next term is 28 – 9 = 19
63 **6101**

3068   4079   5090   ?

+1011   +1011   +1011

So the next term is 5090 + 1011 = 6101
64 **D8F6**
A5C9 B6D8 C7E7 ? The letters are progressing through the alphabet, the first umber is increasing by 1 each time and the second number is decreasing by 1, so the next term will be D8F6.
65 **1046-X**
The numbers increase by 103 each time and the letters move back to the previous letter in the alphabet.

Test Paper 2

1 b The first letter represents the larger outer shape (A is a circle, B a square, C a triangle); the second letter represents the inner smaller shape (X is a circle, Y is a square, Z is a triangle).
2 e The first letter represents the style of the base lines (D is double thin lines, E is solid black line, F is a single plain line); the second letter represents the shape of the 'flag' (L is a triangle, M is a square, N is an indented rectangle).

3 d The first letter represents the number of circles along the line (A is 4, B is 5, C is 6); the second letter represents the shading of the circles (X is all white, Y is black and white, Z is all black).
4 d The first letter represents the number of vertical lines in the pattern (J is 1, K is 2, L is 3); the second letter represents the number of horizontal lines (A is 1, B is 2, C is 3).
5 a The second shape is a reflection of the first shape to make an enclosed shape, the left half of the shape having an inner dotted line and the right half having an additional outer plain line.
6 b The second pattern is a repeat of the first pattern with the number of vertical lines doubled and an additional perpendicular line at the opposite end of the pattern, extending beyond the set of lines.
7 d The second shape is made up of the 2 end circles of the first shape, with the same shading and in the same orientation.
8 c The second shape is the first shape reflected in a vertical mirror line.
9 d The second pattern is made up of the same number of black circles as there are straight lines in the first shape.
10 e All of the shapes on the left have an arrow with right angle turns coming out from a curved shape.
11 b All of the shapes on the left are quadrilaterals with a smaller shape inside and with 1 of the 2 areas shaded and 1 white.
12 d All of the shapes on the left have a zigzag arrow with right angle bends passing through a circle, with 1 of the right-angle bends inside the circle, and with a plain arrowhead with either no tail or a black arrowhead at the other end of the arrow.
13 b All of the shapes on the left are same size squares with a smaller square inside not touching any edge. Three short lines project out from the sides and there is a small white circle on the outside of 1 side.
14 a **Wednesday and Friday**
b **28 mins**
c **84 mins**
15 a is 8, b is 1 7 + 5 = 12, so 1 to carry to the tens column, 2 + 1 = 3, so to make 11 a must be 8; 1 to carry to the hundreds column, 3 + 1 = 4, so make 5 the value of b must be 1.
16 Four million, six hundred and two thousand and fifteen
17 6 000 066
18 6501
19 408 1000 – 592 = 408
20 1 × 56 2 × 28 4 × 14 7 × 8
21 72 180 279
22 c The black arrow does not point to a white circle in net a; the black circle face is not adjacent to the black arrow in nets b and d. The correct net is c.
23 c There are no faces with diagonal lines in opposite directions in nets a or e; in net b the diagonal line faces are in a row so will not meet at a corner and in net d there are not 3 diagonal faces that will be adjacent. The correct net is c.
24 e The faces with the square grid lines are not adjacent to a face with a black circle in nets a or b; net c does not have a face with square grid lines; the black circle face in net d is not adjacent to the black square. The correct net is e.

25 **c** The 6 is not below the 3 in nets b or d, and it is not adjacent to the 2 in net a. The correct net is c.

26 **23, 29**

27 **182** $5^2 = 125$; $7^2 = 49$; and $2^3 = 8$;
$125 + 49 + 8 = 182$

28 **100** The difference is $(5 \times 5 \times 5) - (5 - 5) =$
$125 - 25 = 100$

29 **23 + 7, 19 + 11** (Either of these pairs of numbers will be accepted)

30 **1302.68**

4 5	¹0	0	5 6	.	¹34	¹5
3	7	0	3	.	7	7
1	3	0	2	.	6	8

31 **58.692**

	3	.	6	4	2
5	5	.	0	5	
5	8	.	6	9	2

32 **£234** $\frac{65}{100} \times 360 = \frac{65}{10} \times 36 = \frac{13}{3} \times 36 = 13 \times 18$
$= 234$

33 **£700** $\frac{105}{15} \times 100 = \frac{21}{3} \times 100 = 7 \times 100 = 700$

34 **£126** $\frac{120}{100} \times 105 = \frac{12}{10} \times 105 = \frac{6}{5} \times 105 = 6 \times 21$
$= 126$

35 **a £60** 10% of £75 is £7.50, so 20% is £15, so the sale price is £75 – £15 = £60
   b £24 10% of £30 is £3, so 20% is £6, so the sale price is £30 – £6 = £24

36 $\frac{21}{125}$ $0.168 = \frac{168}{1000} = \frac{84}{500} = \frac{42}{250} = \frac{21}{125}$

37 **a** $6\frac{1}{2}$ $\frac{26}{4} = 6\frac{1}{4} = 6\frac{1}{2}$
   b $5\frac{2}{3}$ $\frac{17}{3} = 5\frac{2}{3}$
   c $2\frac{5}{7}$ $\frac{19}{7} = 2\frac{5}{7}$

38 **28** Substituting gives $(6 \times 8) - (4 \times 5) = 48 - 20 = 28$

39 **9** $9x + 53 = 134$, $9x = 134 - 53 = 81$, so $x = 81 \div 9 = 9$

40 **67** $(45 - 6) + (4 \times 7) = 39 + 28 = 67$

41 **28** $4^2 + (3 \times 4) - 3^2 = (4 \times 4) + (3 \times 4) = 16 + 12 = 28$

42 **65** $3 \times 4 \times 5 + (2^3 - 3) = 60 + (2 \times 2 \times 2) - 3 = 60 + 8 - 3 = 65$

43 **Square-based pyramid**

44 **A (–6,1)   B (2,3)   C (7,2)**

45 **Trapezium**

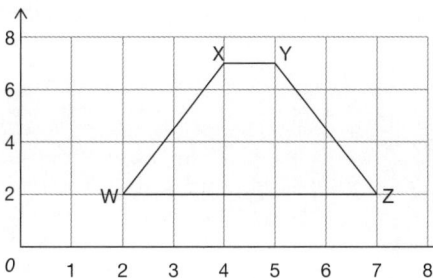

46
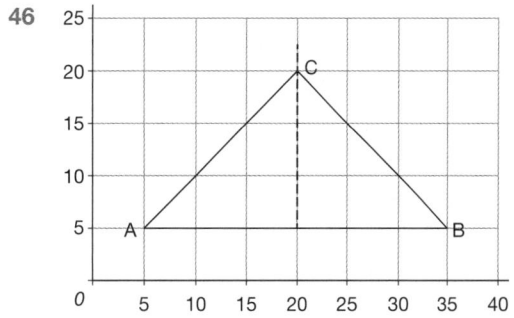

C (20,20) (Point C can be anywhere along the vertical line where $x = 20$, but the coordinate given must be the one that has been marked on the graph.)

47 **1730 mm** 1 m = 1000 mm, 73 cm = 730 mm, total is 1730 mm

48 1.5 km = 1500 m   1750 m   0.707 km = 707 m   770 m
   707 m < 770 m < 1500 m < 1750 m

49 **3860 seconds** 1 hour = 60 minutes, the number of minutes is 60 + 4 = 64; 64 mins = 64 × 60 secs = 3840 secs, so the total is 3840 + 20 = 3860 seconds

50 **72 square cm** The length is twice the width. So the length is 6 × 2 = 12 cm. The area is length × width = 6 12 = 72 sq cm

51 **48 cm** A pentagon has 5 sides; 1 is 12 cm, 4 are 9 cm. So the perimeter is 12 + (4 × 9) = 12 + 36 = 48 cm

52 **1900 g or 1 kg 900 g** The area of lawn is (3 × 5) + (2 × 3) – (pond of 2 × 1) square metres = 15 + 6 – 2 = 19 sq m; the seed needed is 100 g × 19 = 1900 g or 1 kg 900 g

53 **18 cubic metres** $4 \times 3 \times 1.5 = 12 \times 1.5 = 18$ cubic metres

54 **2 metres** 500 sq cm = 0.5 sq m, volume is area × height, so $0.5 \times h = 1 m^3$ and h = 2 m

55 **Train B** time between Tappin and Warton: A is 05.35–06:10 = 35 mins; B is 09:50–10:20 = 30 mins; C is 13:30–14:05 = 35 mins; D is 17:15–17:50 = 35 mins

56 **15:02** 14:37 + 25 mins = 15:02

57 **a 10 km**
   b 150 mins Resting time is shown by a flat horizontal line which starts after $2\frac{1}{2}$ hours = (60 × 2) + 30 = 120 + 30 = 150 mins

58 **4°C** 12°C at 1 p.m., 8°C at 4 p.m., so the temperature drops 4°C.

59 **42** 9 red + 6 blue + 12 white + 15 black = 42

60 **12** Lettuce plants = 3 × 4 = 12; bean plants = 6 × 4 = 24; the difference is 24 – 12 = 12

61 **d** The diagonal lines across the squares in the top and bottom row of the grid alternate in their orientation; in the bottom row when the diagonal line is from bottom left to top right the triangle in the lower right half is shaded, with crossed grid lines shading in the middle section of the grid.

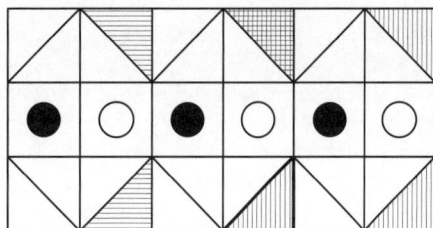

62 **e** The number of short straight lines increases by 1 down the central 2 columns of the grid; the small shapes across the rows alternate between black and white, situated at the top left corner in the grid squares on the left and in the top right corner in the grid squares to the right.

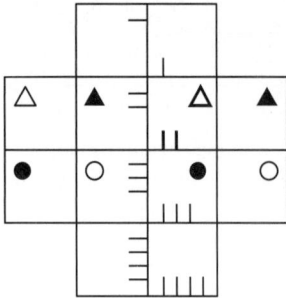

63 **b** The missing square has a larger circle with the same shading as the outer point of the triangle which it is above, that is horizontal line shading.

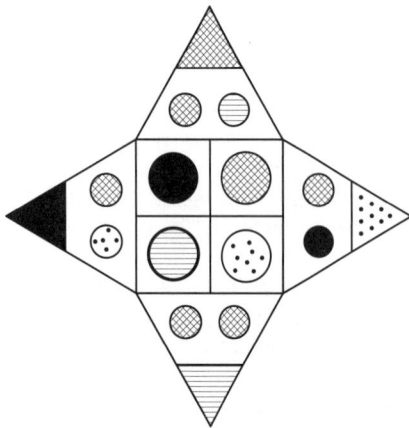

64 **e** The number of black shapes along each row follows a repeating pattern of increasing from 1 to 3 then decreasing from 3 to 1, and then repeating again; the small squares in the lower row are joined together by short straight lines.

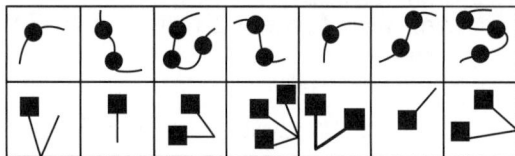

65 **a** **Trapezium (z** is also correct)
   b **22°** Angles in a triangle add up to 180°. 90 + 68 + x = 180, so x = 180 − 158 = 22